basic types of speech

Speech Communication Series

basic types
of speech

Ralph Borden Culp
University of Texas at El Paso

WM. C. BROWN COMPANY PUBLISHERS, *Dubuque, Iowa*

SPEECH SERIES

Consulting Editor

BAXTER M. GEETING, PH.D.
Sacramento State College
Sacramento, California

Copyright © 1968 by
Wm. C. Brown Company Publishers

Library of Congress Catalog Card Number: 68–243(

Printed in U. S. A.

Dynamic developments of our time, particularly the communication explosion and new revelations concerning human behavior, demand fresh approaches to the teaching of speech. Modern life places an emphasis on speech as an *act of communication,* interdisciplinary in nature, capable of adding new dimensions to man's evolution and progress in all areas of life. The SPEECH COMMUNICATION SERIES, addressed to the introductory student, represents a significant attempt to provide new materials for today's teaching needs.

Basic to all titles in the series is the desire to present the material in the clearest and most lucid style for the purpose of making speech communication a useful, ethical and satisfying experience. While the individual titles are self-contained, collectively they provide the substance for a comprehensive study of those topics fundamental to a basic course in speech communication.

For Betty

PREFACE

This book is for speechmakers. Its general subject and approach—speeches studied in terms of particular situations rather than as abstract works of art—is certainly not new. Unlike other treatments of "occasional speaking," however, this book focuses on strategy as much as on tactics. Emphasis is placed on the inventing, arranging, phrasing, and presenting of *ideas and images* to a specific audience for the purpose of self-expression, group coordination, and social control. But throughout, speechmaking is examined in the precise situation in which the speech itself must take place.

Several problems are immediately evident in this approach. Although there are plenty of speeches for each type of situation, there is very little concrete information about what actually happens when the speech occurs. Enough information has been gathered, however, to indicate that every major form of public address deserves a book for itself alone. Even certain sub-types—for example, the "sermon"—are worthy of far more individual study than they ordinarily receive. Yet given the need for selecting a single example to portray a typical situation, it is particularly difficult to say exactly which speech is suitable for that situation. Within a *genre*, variations from type are the rule rather than the exception. Finally, a problem peculiar to this book is the length of most speeches that are both typical and significant. A number of the sample speeches, therefore, while based on actual historical situations, were composed just for this book.

Yet these problems merely add spice to the study of situational speaking. That such a study cannot be wholly new has already been noted. Its antecedents are the theories of Aristotle, as developed and modified by C. S. Baldwin, Lane Cooper, Harry Caplan, H. A. Wichelns, and the pioneer studies of contemporary speechmaking provided by A. S. Phillips, J. A. Winans, C. S. Woolbert, J. A. McGee, and W. N. Brigance. Chief among the book's sources are the *Yale Studies in Attitude and Communication*, directed by C. I. Hovland and others, and the theory of social control propounded by R. T. LaPiere. Anyone writing a speech textbook in 1968 must be indebted to the many excellent textbooks that have gone before and must acknowledge the host of scholarly writers in *Speech Monographs, The Quarterly Journal of Speech,* and *The Speech Teacher,* whose articles have illuminated the teaching of speech in the United States.

Of key importance, however, were the contributions of many friends and teachers. Dr. Edyth Renshaw first pointed the way; Professors Carroll Arnold, George McCalmon, and John F. Wilson helped formulate many of the concepts herein developed; and Professors Angus Austin and Gifford Wingate encouraged the testing of these concepts in class and on the platform. Finally, my students and audiences provided the concrete information about how speechmaking operates in a wide variety of situations.

CONTENTS

Chapter 1

THE SPEECH SITUATION

No doubt you are reading this book because your instructor assigned it. You will find much to quarrel with, but hopefully much that
will help you understand the art of speechmaking. Among the things
you may be surprised to learn is that many men have studied this art
before you. What they have discovered can help you. The place to start
your own study is with the seven basic principles of speechmaking:

1. A *speech* equals (a) a specific human audience *plus* (b) a human
being (c) inventing, arranging, phrasing, and presenting (d) ideas (e)
vocally, verbally, gesturally, and pictorially (f) in a particular space-time
continuum, (g) for the purpose of self-expression, group coordination, and
social control.

2. The speechwright's primary tactical objective is the control of audience attention, and a "good speech" is one to which the audience pays
attention before, during, and after the performance.

3. There is no way to make a good speech without having something
worth saying, without wanting earnestly to say it, and without adapting it
to a particular situation.

4. Preparation and delivery of a speech occur most effectively through
a process incorporating the following stages: analysis of the situation,
composition, phrasing, rehearsal, and presentation.

5. The basic unit of speech composition is *a statement plus necessary
amplification*.

6. The presentation of ideas should be "like conversation" in that (a)
phrasing seems unrehearsed; (b) visual, vocal, and psychological contact
develops between speaker and audience; (c) a dialogue occurs between
audience and speaker; (d) each member of the audience feels the speaker
is talking with him alone; (e) the degree of formality varies with the situation; (f) the exchange of ideas is always purposive, and the speaker's
tactics vary with the demands of this purpose; and (g) only the degree
of seriousness and the circumstances of presentation change from private
to public situations.

7. The speaker is responsible for (a) the validity of his information,
(b) the morality of his purpose and his means, (c) the quality of his

preparation, (d) the success of his adaptation, and (e) the effects of his utterance.

There are nine and sixty ways to use these principles in your speech-making, and every single one of them is right. Our approach in this book is via the situation. Your compositional choices are governed primarily by what your audience believes your purpose and subject to be, and the occasion usually determines what your audience expects.

Long ago it was noticed that there are five general types of occasion:

1. those demanding inquiry and explanation;
2. those demanding persuasion and deliberation;
3. those demanding sociality and courtesy;
4. those demanding commemoration; *and*
5. those demanding counsel.

Within each of these situations you must study your audience and the particular reasons for its gathering. Then you must examine your purpose, your subject, and your proposition in the light of what you have discovered about audience and occasion. Once you have gathered as much information as possible about these factors, your ideas must be arranged in an order that seems feasible, assigned words and phrases, and after a rehearsal period, presented to your audience.

AUDIENCE AND OCCASION

You will not be surprised to learn that people come in all shapes and sizes. An audience is not itself a person, but is a collection of persons more or less psychologically united (if only to hear you). Your task is to become aware of each person in your audience. If you face a hundred spectators, you must analyze a hundred different "audiences."

Although this individual seeks always to satisfy deep-seated psychological and physiological *needs,* his life is governed primarily by ways of satisfying them. He has been taught the proper means of satisfaction, and to these goals he has assigned a *value.* What you seek is knowledge of your listener's value-system—those people and ideas he holds most dear, those things he hates, and the vast range of values between these two extremes. When a person is consciously or unconsciously ready to act in terms of a given value, this tendency to respond is called an *attitude.* Sometimes verbalized, sometimes not, attitudes are usually organized into patterns which are called *frames of reference.* Attitudes and frames of reference, working with and through language, force your listener into a continuous state of prejudgment. Most people will go to any length to make the world fit their view of it.

This view is learned from their families, neighborhoods, jobs, peer groups (class, age, occupation, residence, or what have you), communities, and clubs. Speak to anyone about his primary groups and the odds favor his listening to you, learning from you, and following your instructions.

Each person in your audience is also a "category of the population," or fits into many categories. He is constantly forming social aggregations like those on a bus, in automobile traffic, or in a group of students changing classes. Speak in terms of these aggregates and you will be listened to.

A special problem for you in this era of radio and television is the vast assemblage of anonymous individuals that may listen to a broadcast. These people share the moment of your speech, but they are related to each other only in the most general way. Within the context of certain national or international rules and rituals, and with only their humanity in common, they represent a wide variety of needs, attitudes, and frames of reference. All you can do is aim your materials toward the broadest possible value system that fits the occasion.

Most of the time, however, you will work with groups a good deal smaller than the television or radio audience. You can therefore discover what age levels and percentages of each sex; what educational groups, jobs, and professions; what sports and recreations; what families, national groups, religious affiliations, and political preferences dominate in your audience. You can ask where each member of the audience was born or brought up, and where he lives now. You can try to place him along the continuum from "opposed" through "neutral" to "partisan" in his attitudes toward you and your ideas. You can discover which attitudes govern his reasoning, conversing, and ritualizing. You can understand the ways in which he perceives and comprehends the world he lives in. You can grasp at least part of his unique personality.

The world of most immediate importance to your speech is your listener's reason for being part of your audience in the first place. What does he desire from the situation? We have already noted the five general demands that alone or in combination characterize each occasion for speechmaking. The premise of this book is that we may study five discrete situations in which one of these demands will predominate. In later chapters these situations are developed in some detail. For now, it is enough to observe that you must ask of every audience and every occasion one central question: "Why have these people gathered to hear me; to what extent do they feel part of a unique group; and what influence has the present occasion on their needs, attitudes, and frames of reference?"

The "present occasion" includes a place, a time, and an event that brings your audience together. Analysis of your audience's demands will most often start with knowledge of the occasion. It is particularly important to find the conventions your audience follows when it gathers in this hall at this time. The degree to which you understand and control place, time, and event will come very close to the degree of control you can exert over your audience.

Another aspect of the occasion that may bother you is the question "How long should I speak?" If you have the say-so, the traditional answer "long enough" will serve. But usually others will dictate the time allowed. You will control only your adaptation to the assignment and the efficiency with which you use the time. When adjusting the length of your speech, you should remember that audiences of today seem to prefer speeches that range from five to thirty minutes. Whatever the assigned length, you should stay close to it. You will find that audiences like to feel they are getting their money's worth but that conversely they like nothing better than to have you finish.

When attempting to make the best use of the time, you should remember that only sixty to eighty percent of the available time can be devoted to your central idea. The remaining time is spent getting started, making transitions, and finishing.

THE SPEECH PURPOSE

We have already observed that every speech aims for a unique combination of self-expression, group coordination, and social control. Your audience is induced to want or need to believe and act in the manner you desire. Your listeners drive themselves to perceive, comprehend, and accept the ideas and goals you offer them.

To help you realize precisely what you hope to accomplish in your speech, early in your preparation you should establish the general response you want from your audience. Each response involves a kind of subject-matter. Purpose, response, and subject-matter are related as follows:

PURPOSE	RESPONSE	SUBJECT-MATTER
To entertain, or amuse	Thrills or momentary excitement	Exaggerated or understated "facts"; nonsense
To explain (describe, discuss, inform, inquire, instruct, report)	Understanding	Information without manipulative intent

| To persuade (argue, convince, debate, prove, reinforce, stimulate) | Reinforcement of needs, attitudes, and frames of reference; desire for belief and action | Identification of audience needs, attitudes, and frames of reference with a "prescription for behavior" |

Given these responses, which may be sought in any of the six speech situations, a standard specific purpose for each response is delineated below:

RESPONSE	SPECIFIC PURPOSE
Thrills and momentary excitement	To entertain Dr. Culp's speech class at 1:00 p.m., December 20, 1967, at the Christmas Party
Understanding	To explain the operation of the State Department in a ten-minute speech to Post Number 48, American Legion, at the Annual Father-Son Banquet, Tuesday, July 13, 1967, at 8:00 p.m.
Reinforcement	To persuade the El Paso Citizens Council at its weekly meeting, Tuesday, July 13, 1967, at 10:00 a.m., that El Paso needs a convention center
Desire for belief and action	To persuade the Texas and New Mexico Chambers of Commerce at their joint meeting, Friday, May 12, 1967, at 2:00 p.m., that El Paso County should become a free port of entry

Once you have settled on your specific purpose, you need to answer the question "What should I tell my audience?" In every speech it is wise to announce a goal your listeners can concentrate on. This announcement, which in this book will be called your "formal purpose," should be as close to your specific purpose as possible. But it should be phrased in a manner calculated to encourage perception, comprehension, belief, and action in accordance with your desires, or to cause identification with you or your message.

However you phrase your speech goal, or whatever you call it, you should write it down. With the total situation clearly in mind, you should ask of your purpose the following questions:

1. Is this truly what I want to accomplish?

2. Does my present phrasing accurately portray what my speech will seek to accomplish?

3. If my purpose is at odds with my audience, how may I adapt its phrasing to allay resistance until I can state my case?

4. What demands does my purpose make with regard to audience expectations?

5. What demands does my purpose make with regard to my subject?

THE SUBJECT

Undoubtedly the question heard most by teachers of public speaking is "What'll I talk about?" or "Where can I get a subject?" The standard answer, "Talk about what you know," merely begs the question.

"Subject-land" is divided into three parts: (1) what your audience knows a little about and wants to know more about, and you know a lot about; (2) what your audience has a general awareness of and wants specific details about, and you have a good deal of information about; (3) what both you and your audience are intrigued, piqued, or entranced by.

Remember, you need know only a little more than your listeners to be "worth listening to." You need not have the last, the only, or a totally new piece of information or point of view. In any given population the amount of absolute freshness—of "genius"—is about one percent. But every person has a unique way of looking at the world, a private range of interest, and a measure of maturity that can be brought to bear on the speechmaking process. The essential problem, if we may paraphrase Ernest Hemingway, is to know what you truly feel, what you really know, rather than what you are supposed to feel and be and know. Nothing in you is apt to be original, but the way you struggle with your knowledge *is* unique. What is wanted is a picture of *your* reality.

Yet this is not to say that any subject is valid just because you, a unique person, choose to talk about it. You must question your subjects with the same precision you applied to your purpose. Many questions arise directly from your study of audience, occasion, and time. Others may occur to you only after you have performed a good deal of research, or have proceeded into composition and rehearsal. But somehow you need to discover if your subject is truly something your audience wants to hear about and that you want to talk about. You must determine what you expect your listeners to do when they hear your speech. And of course you must decide whether you know your subject well enough to prepare it in time for your performance.

Preparing your subject is more important than choosing it. The process of getting to know your subject is called "research," and a surprising number of speeches collapse because of failure to find out enough. There are four places to search for materials about your subject: (1) what *you* know about it; (2) what your *friends* (or *enemies*) know about it; (3) what your *library* contains about it; and (4) what your *meditation* on the ideas you have gathered reveals about it.

Undoubtedly your library—in effect, everything written in manuscripts, books, or periodicals; everything preserved on film; and everything expressed by your professors—will provide the largest share of the ideas and images you bring to your performance. With regard to your school's "official library," we must assume here that you know your way around the various sections, the card catalogue, and the librarians. But the following hints may well be in order:

1. Just because material is written, published, or given in a classroom lecture, it is not necessarily *so*. You must question and check the author: who is he, how does he know, what is his point of view, and can he be trusted?

2. Much of the material you find most readily available—in popular magazines, best-selling books, newspapers—is apt to prove untrustworthy because these publications are interested primarily in entertainment or in selling advertisements by means of entertainment.

3. Many of the stories that pass for "news" or "serious commentary" are prepared not by dedicated reporters but by public relations firms that are interested in persuading rather than informing. These articles are seldom labeled "advertisement," but that is what they are. They should be measured accordingly.

4. While in many books and periodicals there is no problem with advertising or entertainment, the content of articles in them is controlled by the political, social, or economic point of view the publication presents. Of both the "entertainment sources" and the "journals of opinion," therefore, you must ask where they stand on the issues of the day.

No doubt these hints could be summed up by the old saying, "Believe nothing that you hear, and only half of what you see." And be sure you qualify *that* as craftily as you can. As a rule, moreover, the wider the range of your sources and the larger their number, the more effective your speech will be. Perhaps only a third of what you have found out will actually be delivered, but its quality will be determined by the two-thirds that remains unspoken. Furthermore, you should force yourself out of the well-known human tendency to read only materials or seek only information you already agree with, or have learned before. It is particularly important that you examine sources alien to you.

About "meditation"—the fourth source of speech material—you may wonder as you consider what we have said about research. No new ideas come from it unless perhaps you remember something long forgotten. Yet the fusion of the ideas you have gathered into a unique point of view will happen only if you put them into your head and let them rest a while. Ideas simply do not achieve full impact if taken from source to audience immediately. You must let them grow and change, and you must give yourself a chance to gain a clear perspective. Only when this has happened are your ideas ready for communication.

THE PROPOSITION

As a freshman once put it, "the proposition is a sentence with responsibilities." To establish what he meant, let us define the term "proposition" as:

a single, simple, declarative sentence, preferably in the active voice, which either phrases the entire subject or makes an assertion that the audience is supposed to affirm.

It is the central idea of your speech, put in a declarative sentence. It is the belief or attitude you are advocating. Not only should every speech have a proposition that is clearly stated and is known to the speaker early in his preparation, regardless of how he handles it in performance, but also *there should be only one proposition for every speech.*

There are three types of proposition: *fact, value,* and *policy* (or *action*). As soon as possible in your preparation you must decide which of the three is most useful to your situation and your purpose. Often one or the other of these factors will dictate your proposition. Once you settle on it, however you come by it, you must ask the following:

1. Is this proposal the central idea or the attitude I want to communicate?
2. Have I phrased what I want to communicate accurately and objectively?
3. Have I stated my proposal affirmatively?
4. Have I a clear definition of all key terms?
5. What demands will this proposition make with regard to audience expectations?

Having answered these questions, you are ready to ask, "What are the issues?" An *issue* is a question that your audience or the logic of the situation demands to have answered before the proposition *can* be affirmed. Any question may be asked. One proposition can have many issues. Over the centuries, however, a number of "stock issues" have appeared in speech after speech. A delineation of these may be seen below:

TYPE OF PROPOSITION	STOCK ISSUES
Proposition of *Fact*	1. What are the facts? 2. How reliable are the facts? the source? 3. What do the facts *mean?*
Proposition of *Value*	1. What issues of fact are there? 2. What value-systems are involved? 3. What values are at work?

Proposition of *Policy*
or Action

1. What issues of fact are there?
2. What issues of value are there?
3. Is there a need?
4. Does the proposal meet this need?
5. Is the proposal safe, legal, constitutional?
6. Is the proposal feasible or workable?
7. What will the proposal cost?
8. How does the proposal fit tradition or custom?

THE ARRANGEMENT

A camel, it has been said, is a horse designed by a committee. All matter consists of positive and negative charges of electricity. Differences in kind are principally the result of arrangement. Thus nothing that you do while preparing and delivering your speech is apt to have so great an influence on your success as the way you arrange your ideas. In most textbooks on speechmaking, you are told that a speech must have "beginning, middle, and end." The first is usually called "introduction"; the second, "body," "discussion," or "development"; and the third, "conclusion." You are exhorted to approximate one of the following three-stage patterns:

SUBJECT-ORIENTED

1. Tell them what you are going to tell them.
2. Tell them.
3. Tell them what you told them.

PURPOSE-ORIENTED

1. Tell them what you are going to do.
2. Do it.
3. Tell them what you did.

Some textbooks, however, have deplored this insistence on logical development. They have stressed the importance of audience reaction in your choice of what to say at a given moment. Phrased as questions in the minds of your listeners, these stages of reaction form a sequence as follows:

1. Who is he, and what is going on here?
2. What is in it for me? Who needs it? Who wants it?
3. Yes, I need (want) it. *How* can I get it?
4. Yes, that is what I need (want). *Where* can I (what can I *do* to) get it?

Your speech, then, is arranged as a series of more or less detailed answers to these questions. First, you show your audience who you are and what you intend to accomplish. Having thus captured audience attention, you then explain how audience needs are involved. Once these needs have been realized, you demonstrate how to satisfy them. And finally, you reveal what action must be taken to achieve this satisfaction.

In this book we will study four styles of arrangement. No matter what rationale you use, you must deal with situations requiring emphasis on information and logical thinking (Style I). At other times you must stress control of audience motives through arguments and evidence (Style II). And though your success in all speeches depends on the extent to which you can coalesce audience needs and attitudes around your proposition, there are situations in which your *primary* concern is the satisfaction of need (Style III) or the identification with frames of reference (Style IV).

Style I.—There are five stages as indicated below:

STAGE	SPEAKER ACTIVITY
Attention Step (Speaker gains audience attention by using ideas and phrases that fit the descriptions listed under "Speaker Activity.")	1. *The Vital*: life and death; hunger; pocketbook; procreation. 2. *The Familiar* or *The Near-at-Hand; The Novel* or *The Far-Away.* 3. *The Shocking Idea or Phrase.* 4. *The Suspenseful*: struggle; conflict; unfinished incident. 5. *The Large; The Small; The Well-Organized.* 6. *The Dynamic*: change; action; movement. 7. *The Humorous.*
Orientation Step (Speaker focuses audience attention on himself and his speech by using one, or some combination, of the items listed under "Speaker Activity.")	1. *Subject*: state it in a phrase or a sentence, using as much detail as necessary. 2. *History and Background* of subject or occasion. 3. *Identification*: speaker with audience and occasion; audience with subject. 4. *Right to Speak*: speaker's sources and qualifications. 5. *Formal Purpose.* 6. *Formal Proposition.* 7. *Partition*: of subject, purpose, or proposition.
Exposition Step (Speaker develops, discusses, delineates, describes, or exposes his sub-	1. *Main Points*: structural units of the subject, *or* points of view toward it. 2. *Topic Sentences*: an entire main point summarized in a declarative sentence.

ject in great detail, using
the devices indicated
under "Speaker Activity.")

3. *Sub-Points*: parts of a main point, or points of view toward it.

4. *Sub-Topic Sentence*: the entire sub-point summarized in a declarative sentence.

5. *Supporting Materials*: facts, definitions, etc., used to amplify main points and sub-points as necessary for perception, comprehension, belief, and action.

6. *Transitions*: word, phrase, sentence, or group of sentences that tells the audience what has just been covered and what will be covered next.

7. *Internal Summaries*: detailed restatement of material already covered.

8. *Indexing Materials*: word, phrase, sentence, or group of sentences that directs audience attention; sometimes called "signposting" or "highlighting."

— — — — — — — — — — — — — — — — —

Summation Step

1. Restatement of main points in as much detail as necessary.

— — — — — — — — — — — — — — — — —

Peroration Step

1. Statement or restatement of proposition.

There are five aspects of exposition that you must consider when you compose your speech. The first is "rationale." You must arrange your main points (or the sub-points under a given main point) according to a logical pattern. Each subject is unique, of course, but over the centuries a number of patterns have appeared frequently enough to be given names. Your exposition step should therefore be arranged in one of the following patterns:

1. *Time*: each point is a moment in time, and the movement of the speech is usually from earliest to latest time.

2. *Space*: each point is a place in space, and the points move in a single geometric direction.

3. *Topical*: each point is an arbitrary part of the subject, or a point of view toward it; some widely-used topical patterns are as follows:

  a. Purpose-Means.
  b. Principle-Technique.
  c. Theory-Practice.
  d. Equipment-Use (or Equipment-Activity).
  e. General-Specific (or Specific-General).
  f. Causal (Causes, Effects, or Cause-Effect).
  g. Analogical: Comparison-Contrast.

    h. Question-Answer.

    i. Increasing (or Decreasing) Difficulty (or Importance).

    j. Problem-Solution (or Need-Remedy) (or Threat-Relief).

    4. *Inquiry*: each point is a question which seeks to open up a stage of reflective thinking (e.g., What is the problem? What does the problem involve? What are the criteria for judging solutions?)

    5. *Narrative*: the ideas in the speech are revealed by means of a story that incorporates all the points to be covered.

Given a suitable pattern of main points, the second aspect of exposition you must consider is "number." Just as there is no magic pattern, there is no special number of points that must always be used. Yet more than five points is apt to prove confusing, and no subject can be divided into less than two points. Though to some extent you are at the mercy of your subject, you should beware of complicated arrangements. There is no reason you cannot impose a simpler pattern of your own, adapted to your situation, no matter what the subject seems to involve. In any case, the fewer the main points, the clearer your exposition will be.

The third consideration is the "problem of series." That is, where should you place your most important point? The evidence is inconclusive, but the following observations seem to be true:

    1. In any series of three or more points, the middle position is the least effective. *Where possible, use a two-point pattern.*

    2. In any series, when the audience is relatively intelligent, informed, or favorable to the speaker or his proposal, the first position in the series is the most effective. *Points should be in ANTI-CLIMAX order (most important point first).*

    3. In any series, when the audience is relatively unintelligent, uninformed, or unfavorable to the speaker or his proposal, the last position in the series is the most effective. *Points should be in CLIMAX order (most important point last).*

A fourth aspect of exposition is "coordination-subordination." All points at a given level of generality should be related to each other in some way; this is "coordination." During the time you devote to each point, only materials relevant to *it* should be dealt with; this is "subordination."

The last and undoubtedly the most important consideration when preparing your Exposition Step is the problem of "amplification." The hardest lesson you will have to learn about speechmaking is that the statements or assertions you use for your main points and sub-points are seldom understandable, acceptable, believable, or cogent for a given audience. You make a statement. If your audience instantly understands, believes, and accepts what you say, you proceed to the next point or sub-point. But if there is any problem in comprehension, you must stop the forward movement of your ideas and *amplify* the point that is unclear or unimpressive. The process of amplification requires you to surround your assertions with the following types of supporting material:

1. INFORMATION: facts and figures, data answering the questions *Who? What? Where?* and *When?*

2. EXPLANATION: data answering the questions *Why? How?* and *To what degree?*

3. AUTHENTICATION: material that answers the question *Who says so?* That is, the *authority* of experts, the *testimony* of witnesses.

4. ILLUSTRATION: specific instances of the proposition "in action." That is, *examples* long or short, real or hypothetical.

5. ASSOCIATION: comparisons and contrasts, analogies, and metaphors, which answer the question *What's it like?*

6. DEFINITION: what the words denote and connote.

7. QUOTATION: well-known sayings, proverbs, maxims, and slogans.

8. NARRATION: anecdotes, parables, stories of any kind.

9. DESCRIPTION: sensory details.

10. ARGUMENTATION: statements grouped together so they lead to a conclusion, as in a *syllogism*.

11. IMPLICATION: *allusions* to the situation, an historical event, or a literary experience; *rhetorical question,* in which the speaker provides his own answer or which the audience itself answers; *implied conclusion* from a series of declarations.

12. DEMONSTRATION AND VISUAL AIDS: charts, graphs, pictures, working models, the actual items being explained.

13. REITERATION: *repetition* (the same idea in the same words) or *restatement* (the same idea in different words).

Each statement in your speech that is not instantly effective should be accompanied by one or more supports from this "speaker's dozen." There are four possible methods of combining statement and supports. You may begin with the proposition, then follow it with your supports; this is "deductive." Or, turning the paradigm around, you may begin with your supporting materials, then present your proposition; this is "inductive." Many speakers, however, prefer to combine these two methods by using a "withheld proposal"—in which one or more key supports appear first, followed by the proposition, which is then further amplified until the audience has grasped it. The final method of amplification—the "implied" or "concealed" approach—is one in which the proposition is left unsaid.

Whichever method you use, you must become aware of "support clusters." Do not depend on a single type of supporting material to do the job. Where possible, the heart of a support cluster should be information. But the facts and figures should be accompanied by illustration, authentication, definition, or association—as needed. Explanation, of course, will often stand alone, but combining it with association and illustration is a standard approach. Such powerful supports as quotation, allusion, and narration serve well as "clinchers" at the end of a detailed amplification. And you should always make extensive use of iteration.

Style II.—With the first style of arrangement you seek "understanding" through "delivery of information without manipulative intent." While this approach can also serve "to reinforce favorable attitudes" or "to induce belief or action"—the two goals of the persuader—usually when you seek to persuade you use Styles II, III, or IV.

In Style II, you continue to stress both the delivery of information and a logical pattern. The first two stages—the *Attention Step* and the *Orientation Step*—change very little from Style I. The chief difference is that, whatever else you accomplish, you must persuade your audience (1) to focus on a single need, attitude, or frame of reference; (2) to seek understanding through inquiry and explanation; (3) to evaluate and deliberate a problem and its solution; (4) to demand sociality and courtesy, commemoration, or counsel; *and/or* (5) to expect you or your speech to satisfy audience needs.

The third stage in Style II—the *Argumentation Step*—changes considerably from the first style. Rather than "expose" a collection of points that usually are parts of a subject, you marshall "arguments"— or *reasons for accepting your proposition.* As a rule these reasons are the answers to key issues. First you select the two or three issues most important to your audience, or most necessary to affirm your proposition. Then you formulate an answer to each issue, in a single, simple, declarative sentence, preferably in the active voice. This sentence controls the "argument" used to develop the issue. Supporting materials are used in much the same way as in Style I.

Despite key differences, in fact, nothing we said about "exposition" is out of place in "argumentation." Yet because of your concern for audience response, which is now more important than the ideas in your speech, you must expect the following changes in degree:

1. You will more likely use topical, inquiry, or narrative patterns.
2. Among the topical patterns, you will more likely use causal, analogical, question-answer, and problem-solution sequences.
3. You will be more concerned to eliminate weak points in your series of arguments.
4. You will probably find it more necessary to use repetition and restatement, and to highlight or signpost your ideas.
5. You will have more occasion to use inductive, withheld, and concealed relationships between your proposition and your arguments.
6. Your supporting materials will more frequently center around "facts and expert opinion"—that is, *evidence.*

7. But your chief aim is to use arguments, evidence, and supports in such a way that "audience affirmation of your statements and their amplification" occurs—that is, *proof*.

The earliest commentators we know about on argumentation noted that "proof" falls into two broad categories. Subsequent studies have both confirmed and broadened this opinion. Where once we stressed the use of logical patterns in ways that appeal to audience motives, today we believe that even such "logical proof" is inherently "motivational." The following paradigm summarizes several thousand years of observation:

PROPOSITION

ARGUMENT   ARGUMENT   ARGUMENT
                        EVIDENCE
      SUPPORTS   SUPPORTS   SUPPORTS

P L U S

A U D I E N C E   A F F I R M A T I O N
E Q U A L S
P R O O F

LOGICAL PROOF   MOTIVATIONAL PROOF

1. Arguments   1. ETHICAL PROOF
2. Syllogistic Patterns   a. Prestige
3. Facts   b. Honesty
4. Authority   c. Expertness
5. Testimony   d. Knowledge
                                       e. Sympathy for audience

                                    2. ATTITUDINAL PROOF
                                       a. Needs
                                       b. Attitudes
                                       c. Frames of Reference

                                    3. STYLISTIC PROOF
                                       a. Use of Language
                                       b. Delivery

Once you have developed and "proved" your arguments as completely as you can, proceed to your *Summation Step*. Here you restate each of your main arguments. That done, you deliver your *Peroration Step*. Here you have two choices. You may restate (or state for the first time) the proposal that you want your audience to affirm. In "Speech as a Liberal Study," for example, Professor C. C. Arnold wanted to prove that the study of speech belongs among the "humanities." He used three, arguments, and his peroration went as follows:

> Is this [the study of speech] a liberal undertaking? Men have thought so, more often than not, perhaps for the good reason that few studies deal so fundamentally and directly with the vehicles of social experience. With or without the blessings of his academic proctors, Man has insisted upon exploring his speech as behavior and as a social force. Apparently, he has believed these studies could spur his judgment and imagination and enlarge his understanding. Perhaps then we ought to change our question and ask: 'Will the college calling itself "liberal" organize and systematize the study of Speech, or will it have the subject studied piecemeal, narrowly, and anarchically in its porticoes?' This is about the only choice the liberal college has ever had since its conception. I think it is the only choice it has today.*

Often, however, the peroration is not a restatement of the proposition, but a final appeal for action:

> With malice toward none, with charity for all, with firmness in the right as God gives us to see the right, let us strive on to finish the work we are in, to bind up the nation's wounds, to care for him who shall have borne the battle and for his widow and his orphan, to do all which may achieve and cherish a just and lasting peace among ourselves and with all nations.

Style III.—Thus far we have discussed organizing your ideas so that both logical pattern and information were primary, and the response of your audience as you speak secondary. In Styles I and II you emphasize clear and separately-stated main points or arguments, direct evidence, and a straightforward approach to the audience.

We now examine a style of arrangement in which you focus *primarily* on audience response. Though information and logical patterns are still important, the order in which your ideas appear is governed by the standard audience response pattern.** We examined this pattern on pp. 9-10.

The first stage is still the *Attention Step.* Though probably this step is shorter than in the earlier patterns, the same techniques are used. You strive as quickly as possible to answer the audience's opening question: "Who is he, and what is going on here?"

---

*Reprinted from *The Speaker's Resource Book*, 1st ed., by Carroll C. Arnold, Douglas Ehninger, and John Gerber. Copyright © 1961 by Scott, Foresman and Company.

**For some of the terms used in describing this speech pattern I have used words popularized by Alan H. Monroe. See any edition of his *Principles and Types of Speech* (Chicago: Scott, Foresman and Co.). The pattern of audience response and the speech pattern adapted to it, however, are both obvious and common enough in many speech situations. I have examined them somewhat differently from Professor Monroe.

Once the audience has focused on you, the speaker, you proceed to the second stage: the *Need Step*. Here you employ all modes of proof —but primarily motivational proof—to arouse, crystallize and/or focus important audience needs. The stronger the attitudes you excite, the more effective your appeal. But you also try to avoid calling attention to your persuasive intent. The subtler and more indirect you are, the better. Your goal in this step is to answer the audience question "Who needs it?" or "What is in it for me?" Only ideas that help develop this "need" are handled in this stage of the speech. As a rule you first cause powerful but general needs to be felt. Then you marshall these desires around a single need for some change in the status quo.

If you do your work well in the second stage, your audience should reach a point of response at which it says, "Yes, I need (it). *How* can I satisfy my need (for it)?" When this moment occurs—and not before if you can help it—you proceed to the third stage of your speech, the *Satisfaction Step*. During this step you proffer (1) means of relieving the strong needs you have aroused or crystallized and (2) a program to remedy the problem in the status quo upon which you have focused these needs. Once again you may use any mode of proof and the subtler and more indirect you are, the greater will be your chance of success. More important, your means of satisfaction should be linked closely with each aspect of the need (or each of the needs) you have brought into the speech.

At the end of Stage Three your audience should be saying, "Yes, that is what I want. *Where* (or *how*) can I get it?" The situation is ready for your last stage: the *Action Step,* in which you give your audience something to *do.* If it carries out the action you recommend, the audience will get the "satisfaction" you have described. The activity you call for may be something like "Write Congressman White to vote against Daylight Saving Time." Or you may incorporate your proposition into a clear and definite line of action: "As the people who will pay the new tuition, we have a right to be heard. I ask you to join me in petitioning our legislature to hold the line on tuition. Sign your name and save your money."

Style IV.—This method of speech composition is so audience-centered that only with difficulty can we even call it an "organization." We presume the same audience response series, but we provide no pattern of needs and remedies to channel the standard reactions.

In every speech, as many commentators have pointed out, the speaker is vitally concerned with "identification" and "rationalization." That is, he wants his audience *to identify with* his proposal and its supporting material. He hopes that his "reasons for acceptance" will serve *to rationalize* whatever belief or action the listener is asked to affirm.

In Style IV, these psychological processes are used to order the ideas in your speech. Once you have accomplished your *Attention Step*—which is handled the same as in the other styles of arrangement—you are ready for your *Identification Step*. During this stage you amplify ideas and images, situations and incidents, with which your audience has identified favorably. In particular you stress those experiences which you and the audience have shared, are sharing (or can share), and will share. Your goal is to create or reinforce a strong affirmative identification between you and the audience. Your listeners should come to view your interests and theirs as "one."

If they can feel that you and they are "the same," then what you believe and want, they will believe and want—at least in the speech situation. When this identification is strong enough, the feeling of "oneness" will tend to remain after your performance is over.

Once the unity is established, you may proceed directly to a *Peroration Step*—if your proposal is one of fact or value—or an *Action Step*—if your proposition is one of policy or action. In theory anyway, if your audience has truly identified with you, it will follow your prescriptions for behavior almost without question.

If you plan a "call for action," however, you will usually interpose a third stage between "identification" and "action." This is the *Rationalization Step*. The reason is that human beings seldom just "act." They usually dream up "reasons" for their actions. Many students of human behavior believe that this need to think oneself "moral" or "reasonable" is so powerful that most human thoughts are merely an attempt to satisfy the need. Man, they say, is an emotional animal who seeks reasons *after the fact*. Whether or not we accept this extreme view, we must acknowledge that a thirst for "reasons" does seem to motivate people strongly.

That is why, once you have captured audience attention and have caused identification with you and your ideas, you should devote a portion of your speech to amplifying "reasons that seem reasonable whether they are or not." The distinction between reasoning and rationalization is simple though somewhat ambiguous. If your friend says, "Let's stop studying for exams and go to the movies. The break will do you good," his reasoning may in truth be accurate. Your general health can be improved by a rest from studying. On the other hand, unless you are near a state of exhaustion, the break will probably interfere with your studies but not improve your health. Your friend's "reason" then becomes "rationalization." He has given you a moral and logical reason for doing what you have already decided you want to do.

Thus your speech can be arranged in four different ways. Your choice depends on the relationship you desire between your *ideas and images* and your *response to the stages of audience attention*. The important thing to remember is that both speech content and audience response should control your arrangement. The four styles of arrangement we have presented may be summarized as follows:

AUDIENCE QUESTION	SPEAKER'S COMPOSITIONAL RESPONSE			
	I	II	III	IV
Who is he, and what is going on here?	Attention Step	Attention Step	Attention Step	Attention Step
Who are you, and how am I involved?	Orientation Step	Orientation Step		
Who needs it?			Need Step	
Who needs you?				Identification Step
— — — — —	— — — —	— — — —	— — — —	— — — —
How/Why does it work?	Exposition Step			
Why should I? (Reasons)		Argumentation Step		
How can I meet my needs?			Satisfaction Step	
Why should I? (Justification)				Rationalization Step
— — — — —	— — — —	— — — —	— — — —	— — — —
How is that again? (Main Points)	Summation Step	Summation Step		Summation Step
— — — — —	— — — —	— — — —	— — — —	— — — —
How is that again? (Proposition)	Peroration Step			
What do you want?		Peroration Step		Peroration Step
Where can I get it (i.e., the means of "satisfaction")?			Action Step	Action Step

PHRASING THE SPEECH

In many respects, although most speeches that fail do so because of problems with ideas and organization, your speech *is* the words and phrases you use. Given the right word, someone may have told you, you can move the world. Perhaps, but stress on wording often leads to the kind of speech we describe as flowery, glib, or phony. This is because the word itself is no more than a puff of air in the mouth or an agitation of the larynx—noise in the atmosphere—without inherent meaning. Such vibrations are *symbols,* not *things.* They mean only what we agree with our friends and enemies to *say* they mean.

Once we agree that a sound can stand for an experience, we have a most useful tool. But it is only a tool. Your job as speechmaker is to use it so that you and your ideas are understood, appreciated, and accepted. As you seek the words that fit your ideas, you should observe the following principles:

1. Choose meanings first, then the words to express them.
2. Establish definitions early in your speech, and at any time your listeners show ignorance of meanings.
3. Always choose the precise word, out of many similar words, that fits your meaning.
4. Wherever possible, use words that answer the questions what? why? when? how? where? and who?
5. Wherever possible, use words of primary sensory experience—the needs, labors, joys, tastes, and trials of your audience—and blend as many experiences in each word as possible.
6. Use figurative words and phrases.
7. Use words in fresh combinations, and avoid empty words, platitudes, and cliches; never speak just to hear yourself talk.
8. Be forceful and vigorous, direct and personal; use action words, dialogues, and first and second pronouns; avoid the passive voice.
9. Avoid unwieldy, lumbering sentences; jargon; excessive erudition or extreme sloppiness; and unnecessary abstraction or generality.
10. Choose words appropriate to you, your situation, your audience, your subject, and your purpose; furthermore, *be yourself on your best behavior.*

REHEARSAL AND PRESENTATION

A speech exists only in performance, but here we can mention only the basic principles of delivery. For greater detail, you may want to consult Bert E. Bradley, Jr., *Speech Performance* (Dubuque, Iowa: William C. Brown Company Publishers, 1967).

Rehearsal.—Good speech performance obviously *begins* with your inventing and your arranging, and it is *further enhanced* by your style of phrasing. But every speaker needs to practice his final presentation *in advance.* You must take yourself through at least one complete performance in which you imagine and practice aloud all the aspects of the final situation. The number of such rehearsals is up to you, but during each one do not stop and go back. Any parts that require special attention can be gone over at separate rehearsals. For example, you may want to spend extra time on your Attention and Orientation Steps, the topic sentences and transitions in your Exposition Step, your anecdotes or your humor, and your visual aids or demonstrations. If you have a large number of complete rehearsals, strive for different phrases and fresh supporting materials each time you practice, while following always the same arrangement of your main points. That is, do not let yourself memorize any important ideas verbatim.

Your first full run-through should come as soon as possible after you have worked out the order of your ideas, but *before you prepare a detailed sentence outline or a manuscript.* Whenever you can, you should phrase your ideas aloud, on your feet, in the manner of the forthcoming performance. Any "writing" you do, except perhaps for a brief topic outline, should follow the first two or three rehearsals. Unless you plan to read from manuscript, or someone demands a full outline, probably you should do as little writing as possible.

And finally, you should rehearse only until you feel "ready." Most student speakers tend either to under-rehearse or to memorize word-for-word. On the other hand, as we noted above, it is possible to practice so much you lose any hope of spontaneity. It will help if you begin sooner rather than later. An hour a day for ten days is usually better than ten hours the day before your performance. Of course, if you plan to read from manuscript you may find you need a great deal of time before you can read aloud with any success. For help with the techniques of reading aloud, you may wish to consult Paul Hunsinger, *Communicative Interpretation* (Dubuque, Iowa: William C. Brown Company Publishers, 1967.)

Presentation.—Any method of rehearsing that works for you is acceptable, and the same holds for presentation. You must realize, however, that success in delivery is determined by the degree to which your audience responds in the manner you wished them to when you planned the speech. You are not trying to look good, sound good, or have your audience say, "What a fine speech!" or "What a great speaker!" Nor do you want the audience to notice your delivery techniques.

Your presentation, in fact, is solely a bridge between your listeners and your ideas. It will help if you think the speech as you pronounce it, fully realizing the ideas and words as you say them. The way to be able to do this is to follow the suggestions set below:

1. Prepare your ideas thoroughly.
2. Refuse to set words and phrases in their final order prior to performance.
3. Use a simple, logical organization.
4. Gather material from many sources, and seek a wide range of viewpoints.
5. Concentrate on making your audience so involved in your performance that actual dialogues occur.
6. Force yourself to ponder what you say as you say it.
7. Rehearse enough to train your mind and body, but not so much that you memorize anything by rote.

Giving evidence of a desire to communicate is also important. Presumably you would never deliver a speech against your will, but whatever your initial feelings, long and careful preparation will help get you in the mood to speak. Having filled yourself to the brim with ideas in a particular area of human activity, you will find yourself strongly driven to share your knowledge and effort. But it is not enough merely to achieve a desire to communicate. You must reveal it to your audience. The following techniques should help you display a keen sense of communication:

1. Choose materials either familiar to your audience or taken from experiences of your own that your audience can identify with.
2. Use narrative and descriptive supports.
3. Speak and move with a high level of energy, but keep the energy under tight control so that a feeling of intensity is created.
4. Phrase your ideas in first and second person, in the active voice, and with direct address to members of your audience.
5. Look at, and recognize, each person in your audience.
6. Pitch your voice on as intimate and as conversational a level as the situation permits.
7. Encourage by your manner and your actual words full audience participation in your performance.
8. Rehearse your presentation in a suitable manner.

Any method of rehearsal and presentation that satisfies these few requirements is satisfactory. When the time comes you must be able to "stand up, speak up, and shut up." Assuming you are fully prepared, you rise calmly when called on and proceed with all deliberate speed to the place on the platform that you have chosen for your "General Headquarters." Hopefully you will have already checked your pathway so you will not stumble. If you are carrying papers or other materials, they should be packaged neatly and held without fumbling. Better yet, they should be on the platform, ready for use. If you plan to use visual aids or give a demonstration, the materials for this should be set up and working. When you arrive at your GHQ, you should stand for a moment, comfortably "at attention," and look at your audience. A moment will come when most of your listeners have stopped fidgeting and are concentrating on you: the moment of "what is going on here?" That is when you begin your Attention Step. Many speakers like to move toward the audience as they begin speaking. The movement can be as large as walking around the lectern or as small as simply leaning forward. Probably you should not move away from your audience as you begin, unless you move toward a visual aid.

Throughout your performance you must reveal concern for your audience. You should be dressed in a manner suitable for the occasion. You should stand easily, on the balls of your feet, hands wherever they happen to fall. Looking at your audience and including everyone in your gaze, thinking about what you say as you speak easily and freely, you should encourage your audience to participate. If you can, welcome questions throughout the speech or have several announced question periods. If you must delay audience questions until the end, call for them during your Summation Step. As you talk, you should gesture and move when you feel like it or when the ideas seem to call for it. Even when using visual aids or when demonstrating, keep full contact with your audience by facing one-fourth toward the visual aid, three-fourths toward your listeners. Most of all, you should relax and enjoy yourself.

Once you have finished, return to your seat with all deliberate speed. You will feel relieved, expended, and satisfied in a way that comes to human beings only when they truly reach other people.

Suggestions For Further Reading

Arnold, Carroll C., Douglas Ehninger, and John C. Gerber. *The Speaker's Resource Book.* 1st ed. Chicago: Scott, Foresman, 1961.

Baldwin, Charles Sears. *A College Manual of Rhetoric.* New York: Longmans, Green, 1902.

Beardsley, Monroe. *Thinking Straight: Principles of Reasoning for Readers and Writers.* Englewood Cliffs, N. J.: Prentice-Hall, 1956.

Berlo, David K. *The Process of Communication: An Introduction to Theory and Practice.* New York: Holt, Rinehart and Winston, 1960.

Blumer, Herbert. "Collective Behavior." *Principles of Sociology.* Ed. Alfred McClung Lee. New York: Barnes and Noble, 1951.

Bryant, Donald C., and Karl R. Wallace. *Oral Communication: A Short Course in Speaking.* New York: Appleton-Century-Crofts, 1962.

Burke, Kenneth. *A Rhetoric of Motives.* Englewood Cliffs, N. J.: Prentice-Hall, 1950.

Ehninger, Douglas, and Wayne Brockriede. *Decision by Debate.* New York: Dodd, Mead, 1963.

HAYAKAWA, S. I. *Language in Thought and Action*. New York: Harcourt, Brace, 1949.

HOVLAND, CARL I. *et al.* (eds.). *Yale Studies in Attitude and Communication*. 4 volumes. New Haven: Yale University Press, 1957-1963.

HOVLAND, CARL I., IRVING L. JANIS, and HAROLD H. KELLEY. *Communication and Persuasion: Psychological Studies of Opinion Change*. New Haven: Yale University Press, 1953.

LaPIERE, RICHARD T. *A Theory of Social Control*. New York: McGraw-Hill, 1954.

McBURNEY, JAMES H., and GLEN E. MILLS. *Argumentation and Debate: Techniques of a Free Society*. New York: Macmillan, 1964.

McBURNEY, JAMES H., and ERNEST J. WRAGE. *The Art of Good Speech*. Englewood Cliffs, N. J.: Prentice-Hall, 1955.

MONROE, ALAN H., and DOUGLAS EHNINGER. *Principles of Speech*. 5th brief ed. Chicago: Scott, Foresman, 1964.

OLIVER, ROBERT T. *The Psychology of Persuasive Speech*. 2nd ed. New York: David McKay, 1957.

WINANS, JAMES A. *Public Speaking*. New York: Appleton-Century-Crofts, 1915.

Chapter 2

SPEECHES OF INQUIRY
AND EXPLANATION

Picture yourself in an audience that has come to hear Senator Everett Dirksen speak on the Constitution of the United States. You know in advance that he is an expert on this subject and that he is noted for his entertaining and forceful speeches. Now if you believe Dirksen plans to propose a constitutional amendment, your expectations will probably be controlled by your political beliefs. But suppose the senator has been hired by your Political Science Department because he is an effective speaker who is an expert on the Constitution. What you will then expect is that Dirksen will deliver a speech of inquiry and explanation that will not recommend changes, or attack other points of view. He will be a creature of his biases, as all of us are, but he will reveal these with good humor, and they will color but not alter the information he brings to his audience.

On the other hand, let us consider your class in "History 1101, The United States from the Beginning to 1860." There you attend lectures by Professor Dates, and discussion meetings conducted by his graduate assistants. Some of the lectures and the discussions will deal with the United States Constitution, on which the professor is a recognized authority. You must attend class, for roll is taken and absence is punished. More than this, you must get a good grade in the course. What are your expectations as you face Professor Dates and *his* speech on the Constitution? Are you different from the person who goes to hear Senator Dirksen? Suppose, to block a natural objection to this comparison, most of the people at the senator's lecture are required to attend by their history professor. What then are the differences in the two audiences?

Or, to take another tack, let us imagine Senator Dirksen a delegate to a convention that has been called to change the Constitution, or to the original convention that established it. Let us further place him on a committee to examine all possibilities for change or establishment. We are the committee and he is conducting the inquiry, or we are the assembly and he is explaining the results of his committee's study. His biases are still evident, but what about our expectations? To what extent, if any, are we different from the crowd listening to Dirksen in the Student Union Building or the students attending the class lectures by Professor Dates?

The answer is that while there are obvious differences, the similarities are more important. In all three situations—inquiry, report, explanation—we expect information without manipulative intent. Yet we demand that the successful speaker present this information in ways that excite us, amuse us, *and* enlighten us. Even when the information is vital to us, we ask our teacher to force us to acquire it.

As you prepare speeches of inquiry and explanation, therefore, you must remain objective and neutral, but you must also develop your ideas in ways that entertain your audience. It is a truism that information is best communicated when it is "sugar-coated." Less often observed is the need for something of value beneath the sugar.

SPEECH OF INQUIRY

No doubt you have engaged in many a discussion with your friends or co-workers, in which you inquired into one situation or another. By raising pertinent *questions* you proceeded to discover what *answers* you were interested in. All such discussions should (and *do*, though not always *rigorously*) follow the plan set forth below:

I. THE PROBLEM-AREA: Here the group or the individual struggles to describe the incidents (and their causes) which made everyone aware that "something itches." The result should be a short paragraph (fifty to a hundred words) describing the "area of trouble."

II. POSSIBLE QUESTIONS FOR DISCUSSION: Once having evolved a description of the trouble-area, the group or the individual seeks to determine all the possible questions of fact, value, and policy or action that seem germane. These questions are written down and categorized as to type. A good practice is to develop at least three questions for each category.

III. THE QUESTION FOR DISCUSSION: From the minimum of nine questions, the group or individual selects the one question which, if answered, will solve the problem being studied. All important terms in the question should be given working definitions. The scope or limits of the question should be established, and any misconceptions removed or clarified.

IV. THE ISSUES IN THE QUESTION: At this point, all possible problems relevant to the main question are brought to light, either deductively by means of categories (ethics, politics, etc.), for which questions are then devised, or inductively by simply dreaming up the questions and then categorizing them. The result should be a series of "questions-in-depth" that must be answered in order to deal with the main question.

V. THE CRITERIA—ANSWERS TO ISSUES: This stage speaks for itself. If necessary and if possible, answers to key issues are developed as criteria by which the final answers will be judged.

VI. THE ANSWER TO THE MAIN QUESTION: Possible answers are measured against the criteria. The answer chosen does not have to evolve from the inquiry, but usually it does. The most effective method is to formulate a complex answer that combines the many subsidiary answers to key issues.

VII. TESTING THE ANSWER. There is no doubt the answer selected ought to be checked in practice before it is advocated. If this is impossible, the answer should be tried experimentally and then, if successful, used in a limited way until it proves itself (as new drugs are marketed, for example). But if testing will take too long or will be harmful, or if the answer is irrevocable once it is promulgated, the group or the individual performing the inquiry ought to study the most important issues a second time. Reexamine the need, meeting the need, cost, harmfulness, and practicality. Give special study to effects. Allow the persons who will be affected to participate in the final decision.

The importance of the inquiry process to thinking and to group discussion seems obvious. Inquiry is the basic method of explanation. Yet when would an audience expect a *"speech* to inquire"? Probably never, the cynic might answer, and point to the inquiry into the assassination of President Kennedy. Nevertheless, the ideal remains the same: an investigative body or audience that is without bias seeking sound evaluation of facts, opinions, and interpretations.

Let us assume the ideal. Whoever is in the audience, he will have been brought there by a desire for unvarnished study of a problem he feels is significant. When you plan such a speech, you should be sure to announce beforehand a topic of sufficient excitement to draw an audience but of sufficient technical complexity to welcome primarily students of the subject.

The *Attention Step* dramatizes the problem-area, reveals the audience's involvement, and explains the speaker's relationship with the topic and the audience. In the *Orientation Step,* you should take pains to show your expertness and objectivity. Emphasis should be on the speech situation as an open discussion that will seek only "the questions." The main question should be phrased, along with as many of the subsidiary questions as there is time for. The points of exposition should be delineated clearly.

The *Exposition Step* should consist of main points that provide the "stages of inquiry." Sub-points develop the analysis of subsidiary questions. If this step is enlarged to incorporate "answers" (or if this is done at any step), great care must be taken to reflect all points of view. If supporting materials are needed, you should emphasize facts and expert opinion.

In the *Summation Step*, the total inquiry should be restated in outline. The *Peroration Step* should probably include a brief rephrasing of the problem-area but should certainly end with a final statement of the main question.

The following outline is an example of the "speech of inquiry" in which only the pertinent questions are developed.

GENERAL PURPOSE: To inquire.

SPECIFIC PURPOSE: To inquire into the operation of the College Bookstore.

QUESTION: To what extent, if any, should the College Bookstore be modified?

TITLE: "Textbooks and All That: An Inquiry into the Operation of the College Bookstore."

TECHNICAL PLOT (What the speaker does)	OUTLINE (What the speaker says)
ATTENTION STEP	The other day you and I lost an important race. It was neck and neck for a while. First we
Anecdote	were ahead. Then the bookstore was ahead. Then it was even. But, as we came into the home stretch, the bookstore put on a phenomenal burst of speed. Our textbooks arrived and it was only
Humor	Thanksgiving. Once again we had our textbooks
Allusion	just in time to turn them in for one-fourth the price we paid for them.
ORIENTATION STEP	What to do, what to do? I'm sure you've wondered about this as much as I have. Maybe you'd like to take some violent action. But after all we're supposed to be students. I think that before we make any decision we ought to look into the total situation. What I'd like to do this
Formal Purpose	evening is "inquire into the operation of the College Bookstore." I've been studying and inter-
Authentication	viewing for more than a month, and I think I can help you discover the questions we need to
Humor	ask. Incidentally, Mr. Smith, the manager of the bookstore, has cooperated one hundred percent in my research.
Partition	What I want to do is go through a process of four or five steps in which we examine the problem area, then establish the main question, then discover the issues to be discussed, and then make recommendations for further study.

EXPOSITION STEP	I. *The Problem-Area*: We've all had the experience of waiting in line at the bookstore
Main Point I	all day, and then finding the books we need are gone. Or of having to return a book, and discovering we weren't allowed to. Or of trying to sell our books at the end of the
Information	term, and getting only one-fourth their value. Or of having to pay a month's salary just to get the books we must have to pass our courses. These experiences have happened so many times to so many students that we've come here to see what we want to do about it.
Main Point II	II. *The Question for Discussion*: To what extent, if any, should the College Bookstore be modified?
	A. "College Bookstore" refers to the bookstore currently operated by the Business Manager of the College, and managed by Mr. Deaf Smith.
Definition	B. "Modified" includes any change in the present bookstore and the establishment of a second bookstore to compete with the official one.
Main Point III	III. *The Issues*:
Sub-Point A	A. What is a proper college bookstore?
	1. Should it include items other than books and necessary supplies?
	2. What size should it be?
	3. How much profit should it make?
	a. Should there be a rebate of either money or trade?
	b. Should books and supplies be sold at sufficient discount to eliminate profit for the bookstore?
	4. How should it deal with registration?
	5. How should it be managed?
Sub-Point B	B. Who actually owns and operates the College Bookstore?
Sub-Point C	C. How are some other college bookstores operated?
	1. What is the cost of their books?
	2. What do they sell besides books?
	3. How do they handle the rush for books during registration?
	4. How are profits distributed?
	5. Is there only one bookstore?
	6. Do students participate in the management?

Sub-Point D

D. What are the bookstore's problems regarding book orders, returns, size, profit margin, goods other than books?

Sub-Point E

E. What, if any, are the present plans by off-campus business groups to establish a second bookstore?

Sub-Point F

F. Does the bookstore order the full amount of books requested by the faculty?

Sub-Point G

G. What is the history of the bookstore?

SUMMATION STEP

These questions about a "proper" bookstore and about the operation of our own store in the past and the present will provide information we can use to solve the problem, "To what extent, if any, should the College Bookstore be modified?"

PERORATION STEP

If we apply ourselves to these questions, perhaps we can end the long lines, the high prices, and what seems to be a lack of service at our bookstore. Our next step, therefore, is to find and report on the answers we need.

SPEECH TO REPORT

The outline of a "speech of inquiry" we have used stops short of "answers." Quite obviously they could have been included. Since inquiry is usually a group effort, however, it seems better here to separate the questions from the answers. This approach also allows us to examine the report speech as a special type.

As a rule, when the answers are delivered as "reports," each main issue becomes the subject of a separate speech. But it is possible to present a report that deals with the total question. In either case the responsibility can be given to a single person or a committee. Having recognized and accepted the questions, the individual or the group provides data that answers the various issues. These answers then serve as criteria for consideration of solutions to the main problem.

The "speech to report" thus generally occurs when the audience expects clear, accurate information, given objectively, with no attempt to persuade. The pure report situation may seem rare. Usually the "information" is only hypothetical, the speaker is unable to avoid manipulating the audience, *or* the answers are handled as part of the inquiry. Yet it is certainly possible to imagine an objective situation and a speaker with no ax to grind.

Given such a situation, you seek merely to expose or describe a process, mechanism, or activity. You may offer as many details as you wish, but your job is simply to get certain data into the record. Your subject, of course, controls your attitude toward the information, your arrangement, and your phrasing. Your main ideas should be organized according to "Style I," and your supporting materials should be more factual than metaphorical.

The sample report which follows represents one speaker's method of answering the question developed in our speech of inquiry.

GENERAL PURPOSE: To report.

SPECIFIC PURPOSE: To report the College Bookstore's problem with book orders, returns, size, profit margin, and goods other than books.

PROPOSITION: The College Bookstore has an established policy regarding book orders, sales, and returns; is controlled in its profit margin and use of profits; has plans for expansion; and contains only goods that have been requested by students.

TITLE: "You Get What You Ask For"

TECHNICAL PLOT (What the speaker does)	OUTLINE (What the speaker says)
ATTENTION STEP	Garry Owen, our chairman, has asked me to bring you information concerning our bookstore.
ORIENTATION STEP	Working on this assignment took most of my time last week. I talked with Mr. Deaf Smith,
Right to Speak	the manager of the bookstore; Mr. Edward Carpenter, the college business manager; and Tom Jones, of the Student Senate, who's been working
Formal Purpose	on this problem all semester. I'd like to report what they told me. In a nutshell, the bookstore
Formal Proposition	has an established policy regarding book orders, sales, and returns; is controlled in its profit mar-
Partition	gin and use of profits; has plans for expansion; and contains only goods that have been requested by students.
(Transition)	(Let's look at the book policy first, since that's what got us started.)
EXPOSITION STEP	I. Mr. Smith gave me a written statement of the bookstore's policy regarding book orders,
Main Point I	sales, and returns.
Sub-Point A	A. Book Orders
	1. Five months prior to the opening of a semester, cards like this one [show it] are sent to every department chairman, who gives them to every faculty member in his department.
	a. The faculty members fill out the cards.

b. The chairman signs them.
2. Book orders (the cards) are therefore in by a date not later than four
months prior to the opening of a
semester.
3. Mr. Smith then orders from the publishers.
a. It takes three months for the
ordering machinery to operate.
b. Books ordered are on campus one
month prior to any semester, unless the orders are turned in late.

(Transition)   (With the books in, what about sales?)
Sub-Point B   B. Sales
                                1. Books are sold at the publisher's list
Explanation   price, on a first come, first served
                                   basis.
                                2. Books other than textbooks will be
                                   ordered, if the order is more than a
                                   dollar for paperbacks, two dollars for
                                   hardcovers.

(Transition)   (Once we have the books, can we return them?)
                                C. Returns
Explanation   1. The return policy:
                                a. Books may be returned for any
                                   reason the first week.
                                b. Books may be returned any time
                                   a course is *officially* cancelled, or
                                   a course is closed.
                                c. Books may be returned any time
                                   a student *officially* withdraws
                                   from a class or from school.
                                d. Books may be sold to the book-
                                   store during the annual "purchase
                                   period" each spring. Prices paid
                                   are those in the *Used Book Deal-
                                   er's Guide*.
                                2. Books may *not* be returned after the
                                   first week, unless the student has of-
                                   ficially withdrawn from class or from
                                   school.

(Transition)   (What about the profits and where do they go?)
Main Point II   II. Mr. Carpenter advises that the bookstore's
Topic Sentence   profit margin and its use of the profits are
                                    controlled by law.
Sub-Point A   A. Profit margin may not exceed
                                1. 18% gross
Information   2. 6% net

Sub-Point B Information	B. All salaries except the manager's, and all overhead, are paid out of the gross.
Sub-Point C Information	C. Net profits are used to support the Student Union Building.
Examples	1. They help pay the mortgage. 2. They help pay for various events.
(Transition)	(Is the size of the facility a problem?)
Main Point III Topic Sentence	III. The bookstore will expand with the enlargement of the Student Union Building.
Information Information	A. Present size: 6000 sq. ft. B. Size needed in 1970: 15,000 sq. ft. C. Proposed facility: 15,000 sq. ft.
(Transition)	(Is too much room taken up with goods other than books?)
Main Point IV Topic Sentence	IV. Other than textbooks and auxiliary books, only necessary supplies and consumer goods requested by a large number of students are sold.
Information	A. Auxiliary books: paperbacks. B. Supplies: paper, pencils, etc. C. Consumer goods: T-shirts, sweaters with the college emblem, etc.
SUMMATION STEP	Thus we can see that our bookstore 1. has an established policy regarding book orders, returns, and sales; 2. is controlled in its profit margin and its use of profits; 3. has plans for expansion; *and* 4. sells only books, necessary supplies, and goods requested by a large number of students.
PERORATION STEP	This information should help us develop recommendations for modification, if we decide any change is necessary.

SPEECH TO EXPLAIN

In this speech you want your audience to comprehend as many details of your subject as possible. You concentrate more on "how" and "why" than on merely reporting the facts. You may require a wider range of exposition patterns, more detailed illustrations, more anecdotes, and more figurative analogies than in the report. You are more concerned than in the report to find colorful and exciting language. The speech that appears below was designed for a class in public speaking.

GENERAL PURPOSE: To explain.
SPECIFIC PURPOSE: To explain the process of protein synthesis.
PROPOSITION: Protein synthesis is a three-part process involved in the growth of tissue.
TITLE: "Big Things Happen in Small Places"*

TECHNICAL PLOT (What the speaker does)	OUTLINE (What the speaker says)
ATTENTION STEP Allusion Authority	Ladies and gentlemen, Mr. Marshall's introduction has given me an impossible task. Probably I ought to let you go home with his "speech" instead of mine. A lowly cellular biologist outside his lab is like an amoeba out of water.
Authority Humor	But you remember how Dr. Culp said, "Begin with something familiar, like 'God, grandmother, and the grand old flag' (or as George M. Cohan wrote it, 'rag')."
Allusion Humor	Okay, then. Let's suppose we're all five years old, and our mothers have told us (in rare unanimity) to finish our spinach and our steak. This "benevolent monster," as the social psychologists describe her, claims we won't grow up big and strong, and go to Rutgers University, if we do not eat our steak and spinach.
	Well, at the risk of being accused of goodness-knows-what, I'm here to tell you that Mom is right.
ORIENTATION STEP Information Information Illustration	Steak and spinach are just two of the many foodstuffs that are rich in protein. Proteins are essential to the health and well-being of all of us. They make up 50% of all our tissues—like hair, skin, and nails. They make up 75% of all the enzymes and hormones in our bodies. These enzymes are necessary for respiration and digestion, to give just two examples.
Information Definition	For many years scientists knew these facts and more. They knew that proteins were made up of amino acids, of which 26 different kinds could be distinguished. An amino acid is a chemical substance containing an amine group NH_2 and a carboxyl acid group COOH. Thus the name "amino acid."

*Derived from a classroom speech presented by Paul A. Klein on April 25, 1962. Used by permission.

But there were things no biologist understood. Why were proteins different from each other if they contain the same amino acids fundamentally, often in almost identical amounts? Why don't people turn into cows or spinach leaves after eating steak and spinach?

Information
Authority

Information

Illustration

In 1958, Dr. Frederick Sanger, of Cambridge University, answered these questions and was awarded the Nobel Prize in Chemistry. He found that even though two proteins may contain the same amino acids, and in the same quantities, the proteins may differ because of the ways in which the amino acids are arranged. For example, if we have three amino acids, they may be arranged 1-2-3 in steak protein, but 3-1-2 in human protein. This made the two proteins different.

The question still remained: How did an organism arrange the amino acids it engorges to make protein of its own kind? How does a human being, or I should say a human cell, take three amino acids—1, 2, 3—and line them up in 3-1-2 order?

Information

Authority

Information

In 1959, Dr. Severo Ochoa, of New York University, answered this question and was also awarded the Nobel Prize in Medicine and Physiology. Dr. Ochoa developed the principle of protein synthesis, which explains the growth of tissues in all living organisms.

Right to Speak

Authority

For the past ten months I've been working at the Institute of Microbiology on the problem of protein synthesis. I worked in the laboratories of Drs. Braun, Palczuk, and Plescia.

Authority

Formal Purpose

Formal Proposition

Partition

Using this experience, and information from "The Structure of Proteins," an article in *Scientific American* by William Stein and Stanford Moore at the Rockefeller Institute, I'd like to explain protein synthesis, which is a three-part process involved in the growth of all tissue.

The process has three stages: (1) digestion; (2) transportation; and (3) development of the protein molecule.

(Transition)

(Obviously the process must begin with the material to be eaten.)

EXPOSITION STEP

Main Point I

Although there are twenty-six amino acids involved in the steak-to-human being process, we can visualize them in three groups—aa1, aa2, aa3.

Restatement	In steak, the order is 1-2-3; in human protein, 3-1-2.
Indexing	Any questions?
Visual Aid	Okay. Here we have a picture of a steak about to be devoured by a Rutger's student. On his arm you see a cut he received leaping through the window of the girls' dormitory. Somehow, steak tissue has to be transformed into arm tissue.
Explanation Definition Allusion	The steak is ingested and chewed. Small chunks pass into the stomach through the esophagus, where they're acted upon by pepsin—an enzyme that breaks the bonds holding the steak's amino acids together. The acids are now running loose in the system. It's riot time, a sort of "Run-In."
Topic Sentence	Step I thus involves breaking down protein molecules into amino acid molecules.
(Transition)	(Once released, the amino acids are transported throughout the body.)
Main Point II Explanation	The amino acids travel into the small intestines where they go through the wall into tiny capillaries. These capillaries carry the amino acids to the healthy cells lining the injury, by way of the entire circulatory system, of course.
Topic Sentence	Step II is just this movement of amino acids to the various cells of the body.
(Transition) Rhetorical Question	(Any questions? Well, then, how are the steak acids—aa1, aa2, aa3—reconstituted into a 3-1-2 chain? How is Step III accomplished?)
Main Point III Topic Sentence	The microsome, a template RNA system in the cell, arranges for the binding of free amino acids into the pattern used by the cell.
Rhetorical Question	What does this mean?
Information Humor	Within the nucleus of a cell exists a chemical called deoxribonucleic acid—which obviously has to be shortened to DNA, or I'd have to talk all week.
Information Association Explanation	This chemical is a double coil structure that is believed to be the "Executive Manager" of all cellular activities. It somehow orders the production of a set of new chemicals within the nucleus —ribonucleic acid, or RNA. These acids can act as carriers for amino acids, and RNA passes from the nucleus into the cell at large. On the way

each carrier RNA molecule combines with an enzyme and a high energy phosphate.

Information
Visual Aid

There is one carrier RNA for each given amino acid. Here in this diagram I've shown only one carrier, though of course there are a lot more.

Association

Out in the cell are the amino acids, waiting like people downtown for a taxi. The carrier RNA's are the cabs, and each one picks up a specific amino acid. For gas, the RNA has an enzyme and a phosphate.

Information
Restatement

Definition

Association

Information

Each RNA picks up its passenger and then makes a trip to another special structure in the cell— the microsome. As I've already said, the microsome is a template system with parking places assigned to specific amino acids. When the carriers park in their assigned places, the amino acids are automatically arranged in the order suitable for human protein: aa3-aa1-aa2.

Association

Restatement

Information

The amino acids join hands, so to speak, and once they are bonded, the RNA's discharge their passengers. The empty cabs travel back across the cell to pick up more amino acids, once again getting fueled in the same way as before. If traffic increases, the DNA orders the production of more RNA. The executive manager may even call for more taxi-stands.

Explanation

As more and more protein molecules are formed, the cell grows larger and larger until it divides into two cells. (We won't go into *that*). More and more tissue cells appear until the injury is healed.

Humor

Allusion

And none of these hardworking little substances ever complain about the foolishness of jumping through the window in the first place. Isn't that marvelous?

SUMMATION STEP

Not nearly so marvelous as the process I've just described to you in the simplest possible way. These charts here show the activity going on in each human cell at a given instant. Pretty complicated, eh?

But fundamentally the process can be understood just as I've outlined it for you: DNA controls the process in the cell. RNA serves as carrier for the amino acids. At the microsome, free amino acids are rearranged into a new protein. Remember, the old protein is taken in, the amino acids are set free, and then that most marvelous of nature's inventions, the cell, works to put the amino acids back together in proteins of a different kind.

PERORATION STEP   We can truly say, then, that protein synthesis explains the growth of tissue. Our "benevolent monsters" were right when they told us to eat our steak and spinach. Lunch, anyone?

SUGGESTIONS FOR FURTHER READING

BRIGANCE, W. N. *Speech: Its Techniques and Disciplines in a Free Society.* 2nd ed. New York: Appleton-Century-Crofts, 1961. Chapter XX.

MONROE, ALAN H., and DOUGLAS EHNINGER. *Principles of Speech.* 5th brief ed. Chicago: Scott, Foresman and Co., 1964. Chapter IX.

McBURNEY, J. H., and E. J. WRAGE. *The Art of Good Speech.* New York: Prentice-Hall, 1955. Chapters XIII and XIV.

Chapter 3

SPEECHES OF PERSUASION AND DELIBERATION

The howler monkey is so called because he spends much of his time shouting his territorial rights to his neighbor, who in turn shouts back his own territory. For a similar reason we may call man the "deliberating animal." Given a problem, he talks it over with his peers. Though he seems to prefer solutions rather than problems—action rather than solutions—he still likes to debate his choices. The debate may truly consider new ways of behaving, or it may simply rationalize action already chosen, but some form of discussion does seem necessary to problem-solving.

The problems common to deliberative speeches have changed little over the centuries. Legislatures and electorates are most often involved in (1) the credibility of speakers, programs, and policies; (2) economic matters, such as taxes and expenditures, proper use of funds, balance of payments, tariffs; (3) national defense—the proper use of military force to preserve or enlarge the country; (4) foreign affairs, including diplomacy, aid programs, espionage; (5) domestic problems like urban renewal, highways, rivers and harbors, transportation, crime; (6) constitutional matters; and (7) various combinations of these problems. The deliberative speaker needs to make himself particularly well-informed on these subjects.

These problems are debated in a wide variety of situations—from the highly-structured, formal legislature to the free-wheeling saloon argument. Although the latter may be more fun, the former is more apt to accomplish something worthwhile. Whatever its faults, the parliamentary situation is structured to limit man's propensity for moralizing—for fighting over absolutes—so that he may focus on the business of running his public affairs. (See Chapter 4, pp. 60-61.) A strict protocol is established and observed. Only one point at a time is considered, and all sides to an issue are given more or less equal time. Though minority views are respected, the wishes of the majority are followed. The speaker is asked to diminish the impact of ethical and emotional proof, and to emphasize logical proof.

What is supposed to be debated are *means*, not *ends*. Unless opponents already share a "moral absolute," or discover one they can share, they can neither deliberate nor persuade. They must fight. North and South could remain together, for example, so long as they were quarreling over economic and political matters. Once the central issue became a moral one—slavery—the Civil War became inevitable.

The legislative situation, whether formal or informal, ideally is focused on matters of practical concern. Your speech deals with problems and solutions important to the audience involved. You may develop, advocate, or deny a recommended solution; you may propose or attack a total legislative program. Whenever you believe your audience can reasonably be expected to seek deliberation of issues, you must focus on appropriate lines of action—concrete solutions to actual problems.

Your main strategy for this speech involves argumentation—the marshalling of "reasons for" accepting your recommended solution (or your point of view, if "solution" is not your goal). In theory your reasons should be logical, factual, and based on sound evidence, though in practice they only must seem to be so for your audience. The classic deliberative speech thus stands very close to the speeches of inquiry and explanation: "to argue," in fact, comes from the Latin *arguere*, "to make plain or clear." You may or may not present all sides of an issue, but you should be prepared to do so. True deliberation has occurred when you persuade your audience to examine all lines of action, but then to follow the one you recommend.

Successful persuasion of this kind is usually the result of a long and involved process that includes meetings, various kinds of speeches, and often a good deal of backstage pleading. The proposition central to this process is always one of policy or action. At various stages, however, you may well have to argue fact or value propositions. The assignment of problems (and solutions) to committees, the impact of lobbies, and the importance of private maneuvering often mean that acceptance or rejection of a proposal occurs before the actual debate. If your speech represents a majority view, you need only state that view, explain the majority position, or celebrate the process by which it was reached. If your audience is predominantly neutral, however, you must stress the reasoning and the evidence that led to acceptance or rejection of the proposed action.

If your speech presents a minority point of view, you are probably doomed to failure. Your one chance for successful persuasion is to link your view to the majority position. A wiser choice may be to eschew persuasion. Then you may simply explain your stand as a matter of public record—a "position paper"—or as a means of enhancing the prestige of your party.

The audience and the legislative process control your speech in another way. If your audience has little or no idea the problem even exists, your proposition necessarily must be something like "There is a problem" or "This problem is harmful." If, on the other hand, your audience is aware of the problem, you may focus directly on a solution: "The best way to stop the riots is to provide jobs for all slum-dwellers who need them." When your audience expects debate on both problem *and* solution, you should phrase your proposition something like "The State Legislature should modify the Texas Penal Code" or "The Texas Penal Code ought to be changed."

The arguments chosen to affirm or deny your proposition should be discovered through a process of inquiry like that described in Chapter 2 (pp. 26-27). Though you may select your arguments any way you want, you must speak to those issues the *audience* considers important. You may even find it necessary to create concern for an issue your audience has ignored but that you believe is vital. The reason that "stock issues"—need, meeting the need, cost, practicality, harmfulness, and so forth—continue to appear in speech after speech is that audiences continue to wory about them.

The ideas and images used to support each argument may be of any type. It would be nice to say that emphasis should be placed on facts and expert opinion. Persuasion and deliberation, however, require the full range of supporting materials. Your listeners may expect to debate problems and solutions, but they will react to the debate in terms of primary needs and attitudes. (The desire for deliberation is itself both a need and an attitude, and the legislative process a ceremony designed to ritualize this human drive.) Thus even the logic of your arguments and the acceptability of your evidence depend on how well they seem to fit your audience's pet beliefs. Though you ought to stress information, authentication, definition, and literal associations and illustrations, you must always remember that even men in a legislative frame of mind are especially moved by figurative examples and comparisons, by narration and anecdotes, and by humor and concrete description.

THE AFFIRMATIVE SPEECH

The howler monkey, being unconcerned with past or future, can get away with merely sitting and screaming in his eternal present. Men are different at least in that they can both visualize tomorrow and seek to modify yesterday and today so as to improve tomorrow's prospects. When *you* deal with these prospects, of course, you may either affirm or deny (1) the problem itself, (2) the present way of solving it, or (3) the proposals to change today so tomorrow will be better.

Let us assume that, unlike Louis XIV, you want to affirm the problem, deny the present solutions, and recommend a new way to remove the problem. Being human, you should have no trouble desiring action of some kind. Your difficulty, and that of your audience, is choosing the "best" action for a given set of circumstances. Once you have passed that very considerable hurdle, you are ready to make your speech advocating a change in the "status-quo" (a term debaters and others use for "the present way of doing business").

As affirmative speaker you bear a tremendous burden. First you must establish or develop the argument that a serious need or problem both exists for your listeners and, if allowed to continue, will harm them in some way. Then you must provide a remedy or a solution that can reasonably be expected to solve the problem, that is practical and workable, that is not excessively costly in either treasure or blood, that is both legal and constitutional (at least in the United States of America), and that preferably will benefit your listeners in some direct way (like more money or less frustration). Any of these burdens may require several speeches, and all of them may be lost in a welter of other issues. Ordinarily, if you fail to treat both problem and solution effectively, your proposal will be rejected. Non-logical factors enter the debate at every stage, however, and no one can say with complete accuracy *what* proposition will succeed in a given instance. But the affirmative speaker bears the *burden* of proof, regardless of what type of proof the situation demands.

GENERAL PURPOSE:	To persuade.
SPECIFIC PURPOSE:	To persuade that the City of Del Norte should establish a Juvenile Court.
PROPOSITION:	The City of Del Norte should establish a Juvenile Court.
TITLE:	"Why Go Second Class?"

TECHNICAL PLOT (What the speaker does)	OUTLINE (What the speaker says)
ATTENTION STEP: Anecdote Association	Last night I dreamed a terrible dream. I saw my son's life flung into a giant roulette wheel. As the wheel spun his voice screamed for help. While I struggled to reach him, the wheel be-

Association	came the chamber of a revolver, whirling round and round. Suddenly the chamber stopped, and the trigger pulled slowly. As the revolver ex-
Association	ploded against my son's head, there was a shower of lights. The giant chamber became a thousand roulette wheels into which a thousand boys were being hurled. And these wheels in turn became
Description	a thousand revolvers. In the massive series of explosions that followed, I awoke in a cold sweat.
ARGUMENTATION STEP	As I sat there in the dark getting hold of myself, I saw a great many things clearly. The dream
Description	had been frightening, but it was, after all, only a dream. What I now saw clearly, though, wasn't
Information	a dream. It was hard, cold reality. There are fifty-four thousand juveniles—children between the ages of ten and seventeen—in Del Norte. Of these, two thousand will be arrested this year
Explanation	for offenses against the law. They will be apprehended, booked, fingerprinted, and jailed. Some of them may indeed be hardened criminals,
Association	but all will be treated *as if* they were. You may
Identification	think this is the way they should be treated and that, anyway, you and your children aren't af-
Quotation	fected. "It's just some kids from the South Side," you may be thinking. If that's what you believe,
Right to Speak	let me set you straight. As Director of the Juvenile Bureau, I have to evaluate every juvenile arrest we make. If you live in a middle-class neighborhood, if you earn more than $8,000 per
Information	year, your children have a three-to-one chance of becoming juvenile offenders this year over any
Explanation	other type of family in any other type of neighborhood. That means, of the two thousand children arrested, fifteen hundred will come from families and homes just like yours. This is why
Identification	I am so anxious to speak with you, the leaders in business and education and government in our city. Not only do you have the power and the
Formal Purpose	influence to help, you have the need to seek help. This is why I ask you to join me in seeking a
Formal Proposition	Juvenile Court for Del Norte. There are three important reasons why we should establish such
Partition	a court. First and foremost, we need it. Second, the costs would be negligible. And third, we have a moral obligation to our children.
(Transition)	(Let's examine these reasons one at a time.)
ARGUMENTATION STEP: Restatement Information	Do we really need a Juvenile Court in Del Norte? A few minutes ago I said that two thousand of our children will be arrested this year—most of

Sub-Point A	them from homes like our own. What will be the disposition of these cases? Well, the first thing to notice is that "two thousand" represents only a small part of the juveniles our police officers will actually observe breaking the law.
Explanation	Wherever we can, we avoid making an arrest because there is no Juvenile Court to handle the offenders. Only if forced by the severity of the incident do we formally charge a juvenile offender. Most of the time the decision rests with the reporting officer, who must make it in a hurry at the scene of the "crime" with very little in the way of hard evidence to go on. For ex-
Illustration	ample, if he sees a kid with a weapon, he will simply take it away and then return the kid to his parents. No arrest will be made unless the weapon has been used on someone, or the of-
Explanation	fender is caught using it. The officer cannot know, of course, why the juvenile was carrying the weapon—what drove him to it or how soon
Information	this motive will seize him again. A study like that of every case would require something like a Juvenile Court, where a qualified judge could sit with a child and his parents, and examine
Restatement	their problem in detail. So we let many a case
Rhetorical Question	go because the city cannot properly handle it. How many of these children, we may wonder,
Rhetorical Question	are in truth one-time problems? How many will simply go to another neighborhood and complete their aborted crime? The second time they may
Rhetorical Question	succeed. We know it's wrong to let so many go without a full investigation, but what really can we do?
(Transition)	(In fact, let's assume we have arrested a child, and booked him. What happens then?)
Humor	You can take pride in the fact that we have im- proved a bit over the eighteenth century, when the simplest crime—stealing a pair of shoes, say
Association	—was punished by hanging. In those days we took the life of a juvenile offender immediately.
Association Rhetorical Question	Today—supposedly in the twentieth century—we still take his life. Only we delay the ending for a while. What do I mean? Without the services
Sub-Point B	of a Juvenile Court, we must send most of our juveniles who are arrested to an adult court. Those who are convicted must go to the State
Information Restatement	Training School, which is at this moment more than twenty-five percent over its maximum. De- signed for 1200, it now has 1600 inmates. Nearly

Explanation	eighty percent of the juvenile offenders who are sent to prison—for that's what it is, regardless of what we call it—return to crimes after they
Explanation	have served their time. To turn this statistic around, eighty-eight percent of our adult offenders have a juvenile record. Whatever we're
Restatement	doing, we're not saving lives. We are taking
Rhetorical Question	them. Are we much different from our predecessors in the eighteenth century? How many criminals of today might have been changed to
Rhetorical Question	law-abiding citizens through the services of a
Information	Juvenile Court? The court in Austin reports a
Explanation	ninety percent "cure" record. That is, only one in ten returns to crime after being treated by the
Association	court. Is Del Norte less civilized than Austin?
Rhetorical Question	Are our children less deserving than those in Austin? If we want to take their lives, why wait
Association	ten or fifteen years? Why not do it now? Instead
Rhetorical Question	of placing our juveniles in the prison with hardened criminals as we do now—to steal the young lives, as it were—why not simply hang them?
Association	Our present system is slower than the eighteenth
Restatement	century, but it is no less cruel.
(Transition)	(Let me give you the history of just one case. Let us call the boy involved *Jimmy X.*)
Illustration	Jimmy is captured exiting from a high school in
Anecdote	which he and two of his friends wantonly destroyed $30,000 worth of property. The two friends escaped, but later Jimmy is induced to name them. All three are arraigned in an adult court. The parents of Jimmy's friends are well-to-do and can afford to make restitution. Jimmy's parents cannot. Two boys are paroled in the custody of their parents. One is sent to the State Training School. At no time is a proper study
Information	made to find out why two boys from wealthy homes should turn vandal, or why one boy from a poor family elected to join them. Or why the two "leaders" should desert their "follower," who wanted only their friendship, when the alarm was sounded. In fact, no one knows exactly who
Rhetorical Question	called the police. Could it have been the same boys who demanded a crime before they would accept the friendship of a poorer classmate?
Rhetorical Question	Could it be the wrong boy has gone to prison? What exactly are the hidden motivations at work
Explanation	in this case? We will never find out because we have no facility devoted solely to the problems
Information	of juveniles. Multiply Jimmy by a thousand, in-

Thomas R. King

Association	crease the damage from the crime a thousand-fold, and you will have the situation that exists in Del Norte today. But not in Lubbock or Austin, in Houston or Dallas—the only four cities in our state that have a Juvenile Court. We need such a court if only because the police cannot do their job and the judge's as well. We need it only to prevent mistakes in handling those most delicate of creatures—our children. We need a Juvenile Court if only because the crime we commit against our children is far greater, usually, than the one they commit against us. We know the dollars-and-cents worth of the school property destroyed by Jimmy and his "friends." What is the worth of Jimmy's life that *we* destroy? And this is not to mention the psychological harm done the two boys who though equally guilty are set free in the custody of parents who can buy off the crime but cannot change the boys' motives. We need a Juvenile Court if only because the children of Del Norte are at least equal to the children of Austin, Lubbock, Dallas, and Houston. The question is, are *we* equal to the *parents* in these cities, who have properly cared for *their* children?
Argument I	
Explanation Repetition	
Explanation	
Rhetorical Question	
Explanation	
Repetition Explanation Rhetorical Question	
Association	
(Transition)	(If we are their equal, what could possibly hold us back? The cost, perhaps?)
Argument II Definition	The cost of establishing and maintaining a proper Juvenile Court in Del Norte (and "proper" means with specially-trained judge, probation officer, and investigating officers) would be about $100,000 per year. This is approximately one dollar per family in Del Norte. The sales tax you recently voted in will provide ample funds. The cost per year is about ten percent of what juvenile crimes cost us now. If the court reduces the crime costs only by this same percentage, we will break even. As a rule such a court does reduce crime costs about twenty-five percent. I think our court would pay for itself.
Information Explanation	
Information	
Information	
(Transition)	(But suppose it didn't break even? What about our moral obligation?)
Argument III Sub-point A	As citizens of Del Norte, as leaders of business, education, and government—as parents—we have a special responsibility to our city and its children. Not only do we get the kind of city and the kind of juveniles we want, but the city and the juveniles are extensions of ourselves. We aren't bad people. We have good jobs, we
Explanation	

Identification

keep our neighborhoods up, we go to church regularly, we contribute to the United Fund, we even vote most of the time. That we are here at this meeting speaks for our interest in the welfare of our community. We are not average citizens, we are better than average. We want, and we have fought for, better roads and parks and schools. Not only because they are desirable in themselves, but also because we have felt this

Sub-Point B

fight to be our duty as citizens. In our work for a better Del Norte we have not discriminated against fellow citizens who are negro, Latin, or

Rhetorical Question

any race or creed. Is Del Norte known as the International City simply because it's good business? Or have men of good will consciously set out to create a cosmopolitan city noted for harmony among many separate and unique

Identification

groups. We are justly proud that here in Del

Allusion

Norte every citizen of two countries and three states under the eyes of El Cristo Rey can have

Restatement

a place in the sun. We owe our juveniles the same chance, for they are our future. We are

Association

their past. We owe them the care and understanding, the protection, we afford all other citizens. The problems of the young are special

Repetition

problems. We have a moral obligation to treat them as special problems.

SUMMATION STEP

And these problems are real, my friends. *Jimmy X* is not a figment of my imagination. There will be two thousand like him in my office this year, and this number is increasing twice as fast as the population. Our adult court cannot properly handle our juveniles. Many are ignored—a bad thing in itself—none are properly investigated, and many are mishandled—a tragic loss to our community. We take their lives slowly but surely. And what makes it so terrible, we take them unnecessarily. The costs of a court to solve our juvenile problems are so small, the advantages so great, we ought to jump at the bargain. But even without the bargain, we have a moral obligation to our city, to our children, and to ourselves.

PERORATION STEP

Del Norte needs a Juvenile Court, and we ought to take steps to get one. We ought to stop playing Russian Roulette with our children. The terrible dream I described when I began this evening has become an even more terrible reality for over two thousand children. We have condemned

them to second-class citizenship. Contrary to all
we say we believe, contrary to all our actions in
the past, we have discriminated against an important group of Del Norte citizens. As our
city grows, and as we grow with it, why go
second class?

THE NEGATIVE SPEECH

When you make a speech denying the proposition—a speech often
called the "Negative"—you have a simpler though not necessarily less
difficult task than the speaker for the affirmative. He has the burden
of proof, but only one general method of attack. Your strategy as negative
speaker, however, includes several approaches. First you may either
deny or affirm the need. In a denial you develop a proposition like "No
such problem exists here" or "This problem is insignificant, if it exists
at all." If you affirm the need, you may (1) destroy the solution by show-
ing how impractical, harmful, or costly it is; (2) show the link between
solution and problem to be fallacious; (3) argue that the present method
of solving the problem is satisfactory; or (4) offer a counter-proposal
that fits the need. At any stage you may attack the affirmative on any
issue important to the audience (including its peculiar rules of procedure
and the *ethos* of the speaker for the affirmative). Whichever attack you
employ, you should probably choose a proposition of fact or value.
Your arguments should focus on the weakest point in the affirmative
case, and generally you should concentrate on a key affirmative argument or a vital piece of evidence. That is, you should not dissipate your
effect by attacking everything your opponent says. The one best method,
if there is any such, is to show how the affirmative arguments or the
evidence supporting them actually prove the opposite proposition. And
finally, as you marshall your own supports, you should pay special attention to audience needs and involvement in the problem or the solution
being offered.

GENERAL PURPOSE:	To persuade.
SPECIFIC PURPOSE:	To persuade that the continued good health of the American people requires easy access to pharmaceutical vitamins and food supplements.
PROPOSITION:	The continued good health of the American people requires easy access to pharmaceutical vitamins and food supplements.
TITLE:	"Freedom from Hunger"

| TECHNICAL PLOT | OUTLINE |
| (What the speaker does) | (What the speaker says) |

ATTENTION STEP

ORIENTATION STEP
Explanation

Association
Explanation

Information

Information

Explanation

Formal Proposition

Formal Purpose

Partition

(Transition)

ARGUMENTATION STEP
Argument I

Association

Authentication

Information

In the greatest nation on earth, the most successful and prosperous nation in the history of the world, men, women, and children go to bed hungry every night.

I don't mean the very poor, who have nothing to eat. I don't mean the kind of belly-growling hunger so many of us remember from the Hoovervilles of the nineteen thirties. This new kind of hunger is unseen and unfelt—until disease strikes, or examination reveals an alarming percentage of our youth cannot measure up to the army's physical standards and our middle-aged are dying because their bodies are worn out before their time, or the condition of those young men whom the army declares "fit" is such that they cannot keep up with a Viet Cong peasant who eats one cup of rice a day, supplemented by one piece of fish every other day. No, I'm talking about our body's hunger for vitamins and minerals. You and I may eat seventy tons of food during our lifetimes. In this seventy tons is a cupful of invisible chemicals without which we will starve to death no matter how much food we eat. I'm talking about freedom from hunger in the midst of plenty. It seems to me the proponents of the present resolution [bill, proposition] have overlooked both the cupful of value in our lifetime supply of food and the American right to "freedom from hunger." Let me show you what I mean, using information from the very same people who made the present resolution. Let me show you the inadequacies in our diet and the important ways of removing these inadequacies.

(First, there are the administration's [affirmative's, my opponent's] own facts about the inadequacies.)

These facts lead to but one conclusion: many Americans receive an inadequate supply of vitamins and minerals, which one food processor has not very originally called the "building blocks of life." Both the National Research Council and the United States Department of Agriculture tell us, for example, that probably over eighty percent of our boys and girls do not receive vitamins

Explanation

Rhetorical Question

Restatement

Sub-Point A
Visual Aid

Information
Visual Aid

Information

Information
(Transition)

Sub-Point B
Illustration
Explanation

Illustration
Explanation

Authentication

Information

Information
Information
Anecdote

and minerals in amounts equal to the minimum daily requirement. In years to come this hidden hunger, this absence of the building blocks, could lead to poor eyesight and hearing, less than normal strength and coordination, and susceptibility to disease. But does this one example prove that the general American diet is lacking these building blocks? There is more than a possibility—there is a distinct probability—that these necessary food supplements are missing. Five important facts make me say this. *One*: Very little of our perishable food comes to us in less than three days. Here on this chart [show chart] is a diagram of the reduction in food value day by day after harvesting. You will note a fifty percent loss in three days. This carrot [show carrot], for example, is three days old and looks great. It tastes great, too. [Take bite from carrot.] On the other hand, *this* carrot [show second carrot] is fifteen years old. I don't think I'll take a bite out of it. The strange but true fact, however, is that even though these two carrots look different, and one certainly seems more appetizing and nourishing than the other, *they have the same amount of vitamins and minerals.*

(But, you say, that is only perishable foods. Aren't most foods processed right after harvest?)

Two: Food processing does almost as much damage, if not more, than leaving perishable food alone. Raw sugar, for example, is rich in iron. We process it to molasses, which is also rich in iron. We feed the molasses to our cattle and use the refined sugar ourselves. Refined sugar has *no* vitamins or minerals. Another example is wheat. Now wheat is a whole food. We can exist on wheat alone. But first we remove the bran and feed it to our animals. Then we remove the middlings and feed it to our cattle. Then we remove the wheat germ—the heart of the wheat—rich in B-vitamins and in Vitamin E. The remains, farina, is screened. What we now have is unbleached white flour, which according to the Department of Commerce, constitutes ninety-three percent of the flour manufactured in the United States. By this point in the process, some eighteen known vitamins and minerals have been removed. Now I know the flour is then bleached and enriched with some four or five food elements. This reminds me of the man who was

Humor

(Transition)

Rhetorical Question

Rhetorical Question

Visual Aid

Rhetorical Question
Sub-Point C

(Transition)

Sub-Point D
Authentication
Information

Visual Aid
Information

Information

(Transition)

Sub-Point E

Identification

Authentication

Information

held up and robbed. When the thief realized his victim had only eighteen dollars, he gave him back four or five. The man who had been robbed then ran to the police crying: "I'm enriched, I'm enriched!"

(But suppose all the food available still had its vitamins and minerals. Would we then get all the food value we need?)

Let me answer this question with another one. Can any of you name all the vitamins and minerals you need, and the foods that might have them, without looking at a long and involved checklist? How many of you would carry this list of food values [show long list] to every meal at home or at a restaurant? How many of your wives carry this list to the store when they go shopping? Number *Three*, then, of the facts about our inadequate diet is the obvious difficulty we would have selecting the right foods if there were any.

(But even if we could select them without trouble, what happens when we cook them?)

Four: The United States Department of Agriculture confirms that "cooking often takes a heavy toll of vitamins and minerals before the food reaches the table." Here are some more Department of Agriculture charts recording these food values that are lost [show charts]. Just taking a sample survey, we find the following losses: Vitamin C, fifty-eight percent; Niacin, twenty-nine percent; Thiamin, twenty percent; Calcium, forty percent; Phosphorus, fifty-one percent; Iron, twenty-eight percent.

(But I don't need to continue. In a few minutes, I'll have the clerk [secretary] distribute some pamphlets that tell the whole story. There's one more fact about our inadequate diet which I must talk about.)

Five: The fact may be painful, but many of us here—many Americans—have food preferences that are definitely harmful. Last week [this morning] I made an informal study of the members of this house [participants in this tournament]. I found about a third have only coffee and toast for breakfast—the meal that should be the largest and most nutritious. Another third have only a sandwich for lunch—the meal that should be the second largest and the second

most nutritious. And a final third eat no breakfast and no lunch, but have a huge supper—the
Allusion   meal that should be the lightest. And this is not
to mention our preference for soft drinks, candy,
and high-calorie, low-food value desserts.

(Transition)   (These food preferences, plus vitamin-and-min-
eral losses resulting from decay and storage,
Internal Summary   processing, improper selection of food, and preparation and cooking, lead me to state that many
Americans receive an inadequate supply of vitamins and minerals—the building blocks of life—
from the natural foods they eat. The next question is: What can be done about these inadequate
diets?)

If the food we eat cannot keep us healthy, there
Argument II   is only one action we can take. We can select a
good food supplement to eliminate the guess-
work in our diet. By "good food supplement," I
Definition   mean one that contains all the vitamins and
Explanation   minerals we know are required for good health.
These food elements are combined and balanced
just as they are in natural foods before man's
processing and selection alter the balance or
eliminate the vitamins and minerals altogether.
Information   No one can argue without hedging that such a
food supplement is absolutely essential. Let's ad-
Association   mit that. But no one can argue with absolute
certainty—or even partial certitude—that such a
food supplement is *not* necessary. The only thing
Information   we know is that the vitamins and minerals are
necessary. The guesswork lies in figuring out
Restatement   whether the foods we eat—in the ways we Americans customarily eat them—can supply these
necessary vitamins and minerals. We have little
Association   control over natural food values. We *can* control
Summation Step   our food supplements. The question before this
assembly [question for discussion] is not whether
we should all use a food supplement, but whether
we should be forced *not* to use it. The facts I
have shown you reveal that we need vitamins
and minerals, but that our normal diet probably
does not supply them in the proper amounts.
The facts also indicate—and those proposing this
restriction on our health have admitted—that food
supplements can provide the necessary vitamins
and minerals in the proper balance and arrangement for the best of health.

Peroration Step   The American people have become the healthiest
people on earth by choosing their foods and food
supplements without restrictions other than the

normal control of quality and advertising. The
continued good health of the American people
requires this same easy access to pharmaceutical
vitamins and food supplements. Why not continue to keep the guesswork out of our diets?

THE POSITION PAPER

In any deliberative situation the time may come when your proposition has no hope of succeeding. You represent a minority too small to
count, for example, or the legislative process has finished with the question before the group and you have been defeated. The democratic thing
to do is surrender to the inevitable.

Sometimes, however, the issue may seem primarily one of conscience.
Despite the impossibility of legislative success, you may want to speak
out. You may want to declare your position for the public record.

There are at least four approaches you may use. First, you may
simply reiterate the negative point of view which was previously advocated. Second, you may ask your audience to share a vision of how
things will be under the successful legislation. (This may also be a
restatement of points already made.) Third, you may speak in support
of an idea your audience holds in high regard but has set aside tem-
porarily under the impact of the affirmative case. Fourth, you may amplify a value your audience believes in but heretofore has not associated
with the proposal before the group.

The following speech combines the third and the fourth approach.
It was delivered by Senator Robert M. La Follette on June 15, 1917, in
the midst of a terrible war hysteria. As you may note, the speech does
not seem out of place today.

GENERAL PURPOSE: To persuade.
SPECIFIC PURPOSE: To persuade that stifling free speech in wartime is harmful.

PROPOSITION: Stifling free speech in wartime harms the country, the
war effort, and the peace to come.

TITLE: "Free Speech in Wartime"*

TECHNICAL PLOT	OUTLINE
(What the speaker does)	(What the speaker says)
ATTENTION STEP	MR. PRESIDENT: I rise to a question of per- sonal privilege.

---

*The text used is taken from A. Craig Baird (ed.), *American Public Addresses*
1740-1952, in the *McGraw-Hill Series in Speech*, consulting ed. Clarence T. Simon
(New York: McGraw-Hill Book Company, Inc., 1956), pp. 244-248. Used by permission.

I have no intention of taking the time of the Senate with a review of the events which led to our entrance into the war except in so far as they bear upon the question of personal privilege to which I am addressing myself.

IDENTIFICATION STEP

Main Point I

Six Members of the Senate and fifty Members of the House voted against the declaration of war. Immediately there was let loose upon those Senators and Representatives a flood of invective and abuse from newspapers and individuals who had been clamoring for war, unequaled, I believe, in the history of civilized society.

Sub-Point A

Prior to the declaration of war every man who had ventured to oppose our entrance into it had been condemned as a coward or worse, and even the President had by no means been immune from these attacks.

Sub-Point B

Since the declaration of war the triumphant war press has pursued those Senators and Representatives who voted against war with malicious falsehood and recklessly libelous attacks, going to the extreme limit of charging them with treason against their country.

Main Point II

This campaign of libel and character assassination directed against the Members of Congress who opposed our entrance into the war has been continued down to the present hour, and I have upon my desk newspaper clippings, some of them libels upon me alone, some directed as well against other Senators who voted in opposition to the declaration of war. One of these newspaper reports most widely circulated represents a Federal judge in the state of Texas as saying, in a charge to a grand jury—I read the article as it appeared in the newspaper and the headline with which it is introduced:

Illustration

Quotation

DISTRICT JUDGE WOULD LIKE TO TAKE SHOT AT TRAITORS IN CONGRESS
(By Associated Press leased wire)
Houston, Texas, October 1, 1917.
Judge Waller T. Burns, of the United States district court, in charging a Federal grand jury at the beginning of the October term today, after calling by name Senators Stone of Missouri, Hardwick of Georgia, Vardaman of Mississippi, Gronna of North Dakota, Gore of Oklahoma, and LaFollette of Wisconsin, said:

"If I had a wish, I would wish that you men had jurisdiction to return bills of indictment against these men. They ought to be tried promptly and fairly, and I believe this court could administer the law fairly; but I have a conviction, as strong as life, that this country should stand them up against an adobe wall tomorrow and give them what they deserve. If any man deserves death, it is a traitor. I wish that I could pay for the ammunition. I would like to attend the execution, and if I were in the firing squad I would not want to be the marksman who had the blank shell."

. . .

(Transition)

If this newspaper clipping were a single or exceptional instance of lawless defamation, I should not trouble the Senate with a reference to it. But, Mr. President, it is not.

Main Point III

In this mass of newspaper clippings which I have here upon my desk, and which I shall not trouble the Senate to read unless it is desired, and which represent but a small part of the accumulation clipped from the daily press of the country in the last three months, I find other Senators, as well as myself, accused of the highest crimes of which any man can be guilty—treason and disloyalty—and, sir, accused not only with no evidence to support the accusation, but without the suggestion that such evidence anywhere exists. It is not claimed that Senators who opposed the declaration of war have since that time acted with any concerted purpose either regarding war measures or any others. They have voted according to their individual opinions, have often been opposed to each other on bills which have come before the Senate since the declaration of war, and, according to my recollection, have never all voted together since that time upon any single proposition upon which the Senate has been divided.

Sub-Point A

Explanation

Sub-Point B

I am aware, Mr. President, that in pursuance of this campaign of vilification and attempted intimidation, requests from various individuals and certain organizations have been submitted to the Senate for my expulsion from this body, and that such requests have been referred to and considered by one of the committees of the Senate. If I alone had been made the victim of these

Sub-Point C

(Transition)

Main Point IV

Explanation

Information

Illustration

Sub-Point A

Sub-Point B

RATIONALIZATION STEP

Main Point I

attacks, I should not take one moment of the Senate's time for their consideration, and I believe that other Senators who have been unjustly and unfairly assailed, as I have been, hold the same attitude upon this that I do. *Neither the clamor of the mob nor the voice of power will ever turn me by the breadth of a hair from the course I mark out for myself, guided by such knowledge as I can obtain and controlled and directed by a solemn conviction of right and duty.*

But, sir, it is not alone Members of Congress that the war party in this country has sought to intimidate. The mandate seems to have gone forth to the sovereign people of this country that they must be silent while those things are being done by their Government which most vitally concern their well-being, their happiness, and their lives. Today and for weeks past honest and law-abiding citizens of this country are being terrorized and outraged in their rights by those sworn to uphold the laws and protect the rights of the people. I have in my possession numerous affidavits establishing the fact that people are being unlawfully arrested, thrown into jail, held incommunicado for days, only to be eventually discharged without ever having been taken into court, because they have committed no crime. Private residences are being invaded, loyal citizens of undoubted integrity and probity arrested, cross-examined, and the most sacred constitutional rights guaranteed to every American citizen are being violated. It appears to be the purpose of those conducting this campaign to throw the country into a state of terror, to coerce public opinion, to stifle criticism, and suppress discussion of the great issues involved in this war.

I think all men recognize that in time of war the citizen must surrender some rights for the common good which he is entitled to enjoy in time of peace. *But, sir, the right to control their own Government according to constitutional forms is not one of the rights that the citizens of this country are called upon to surrender in time of war.*

Rather in time of war the citizen must be more alert to the preservation of his right to control his government. He must be most watchful of the encroachment of the military upon the civil

Main Point II	power. He must beware of those precedents in support of arbitrary action by administration officials which, excused on the plea of necessity in war time, become the fixed rule when the necessity has passed and normal conditions have been restored.
Main Point III	More than all, the citizen and his representative in Congress in time of war must maintain his right of free speech. More than in times of peace it is necessary that the channels for free public discussion of governmental policies shall be open and unclogged. I believe, Mr. President, that I am now touching upon the most important question in this country today—and that is the right
Explanation	of the citizens of this country and their representatives in Congress to discuss in an orderly way frankly and publicly and without fear, from the platform and through the press, every important phase of this war; its causes, and manner in which it should be conducted, and the terms upon which peace should be made. The belief which is becoming widespread in this land that this most fundamental right is being denied to the citizens of this country is a fact, the tremendous significance of which those in authority
Restatement	have not yet begun to appreciate. I am contending, Mr. President, for the great fundamental right of the sovereign people of this country to make their voice heard and have that voice heeded upon the great questions arising out of this war, including not only how the war shall be prosecuted but the conditions upon which it may be terminated with a due regard for the rights and the honor of this Nation and the interests of humanity.
Formal Proposition	I am contending for this right because the exercise of it is necessary to the welfare, to the existence, of this Government, to the successful conduct of this war, and to a peace which shall be enduring and for the best interest of this country.
PERORATION STEP	Suppose success attends the attempt to stifle all discussion of the issues of this war, all discussions of the terms upon which it should be concluded, all discussion of the objects and purposes to be accomplished by it, and concede the demand of
Rhetorical Question	the war-mad press and war extremists that they monopolize the right of public utterance upon these questions unchallenged, what think you would be the consequences to this country not only during the war but after the war?

Mr. President, our Government, above all others, is founded on the right of the people freely to discuss all matters pertaining to their Government, in war not less than in peace. It is true, sir, that Members of the House of Representatives are elected for two years, the President for four years, and the Members of the Senate for six years, and during their temporary official terms these officers constitute what is called the Government. But back of them always is the controlling sovereign power of the people, and when the people can make their will known, the faithful officer will obey that will. Though the right of the people to express their will by ballot is suspended during the term of office of the elected official, nevertheless the duty of the official to obey the popular will continues throughout his entire term of office. How can that popular will express itself between elections except by meetings, by speeches, by publications, by petitions, and by addresses to the representatives of the people? Any man who seeks to set a limit upon those rights, whether in war or peace, aims a blow at the most vital part of our Government. And then as the time for election approaches and the official is called to account for his stewardship—not a day, not a week, not a month, before the election, but a year or more before it, if the people choose— they must have the right to the freest possible discussion of every question upon which their representative has acted, of the merits of every measure he has supported or opposed, of every vote he has cast and every speech that he has made. And before this great fundamental right every other must, if necessary, give way, for in no other manner can representative government be preserved.

Suggestions For Further Reading

Cooper, Lane. *The Rhetoric of Aristotle*. New York: Appleton-Century-Crofts, Inc., 1932.

Goodrich, Chauncey A. *Select British Eloquence*. Indianapolis, Indiana: The Bobbs-Merrill Co., 1963.

Ehninger, Douglas, and Wayne Brockriede. *Decision by Debate*. New York: Dodd, Mead and Co., 1963.

McBurney, James H., and Glen E. Mills. *Argumentation and Debate: Techniques of a Free Society*. 2nd ed. New York: The Macmillan Co., 1964.

Wrage, Ernest J., and Barnet Baskerville (eds.). *Contemporary Forum: American Speeches on Twentieth-Century Issues*. New York: Harper and Row, 1962.

Chapter 4

SPEECHES OF SOCIALITY
AND COURTESY

This kind of address may strike you as peculiar. As everyone knows many human utterances are *neither true nor false*. Exclamations, commands, questions, and declarations about imaginary situations—these usually are not the concern of the speechmaker. He must focus on declarations about reality that may be *either true or false*.

Yet there is a speech situation which very nearly destroys this convenient dichotomy. You are certainly aware that much human speech is designed only to ameliorate private or social conditions in which we find ourselves from time to time. A conversation like

> How're you?—Fine. How're you doing?—Pretty good. Nice weather we're having.—Yeah. I could stand days like this all the time.—Hope we get some rain pretty soon.—Sure would help. Be seeing you.—Right. Take it easy.

is not concerned with either the welfare of the speakers or the weather. It is simply a courtesy to acknowledge another human being, to announce your own humanity, and to embellish the situation only enough to encourage sociality.

It is only a short step to more formal situations of sociality and courtesy. The chairman of a meeting, for example, or the leader of any kind of group, must speak continually to reinforce the bonds that hold the group together. It is normal for the speaker of the evening or the major contributor to a group's discussion of its needs to be introduced by an officer of the group or by some person directly assigned to the task of creating an atmosphere of acceptance. It is seldom acceptable to present awards, or receive them; to welcome an individual, or respond to such a welcome, without making a formal speech. Whatever may be an individual member's grousing about these situations and the traditional ways of handling them, or the general triteness of such speeches, human groups seem to feel a need for them.

These days, also, many organizations feel a need for the goodwill talk. This is a speech that ostensibly seeks to bring information to an audience, but that actually strives to reinforce or create favorable attitudes toward some institution, practice, or profession. Facts are skillfully blended with indirect arguments and subtle appeals. Business firms, public institutions, schools, churches, and indeed any large organization utilize goodwill speeches as a major item in their public relations activities.

CHAIRMAN'S REMARKS

It has been well established that discussions and meetings function better when they have a leader. The rules of parliamentary procedure center on an effective presiding officer. As Will Rogers is supposed to have said, "Whenever two Americans meet on the street, one of them pounds a gavel and calls the meeting to order."

What must such an officer do—or, for our purposes, *say?* The first step in his preparation is to familiarize himself with the rules of parliamentary law. The standard source is Henry M. Robert, *Rules of Order Revised*, 75th anniversary edition (Chicago: Scott, Foresman and Co., 1951). Special emphasis should be given the nature, purpose, and precedence of commonly-used motions, and the standard form should be compared with the constitution, by-laws, or customs of the group to be led. With this knowledge to build on, the chairman must perform the following:

1. Plan the meeting (purpose, subject or agenda, and facilities).
2. Start on time, and keep the meeting moving briskly and effectively forward.
3. Guide the participation so that (a) hasty, ill-considered action is avoided; (b) each member is given equal time to be heard; (c) the will of the majority is carried out; and (d) the rights of minorities are protected.
4. Maintain impartiality.
5. Speak only when necessary, but make these remarks clearly, forcefully, and courteously.

With certain modifications, the chairman should follow the standard order of business, or the agenda the group has agreed on. The pattern a meeting follows can be memorized as "C-R-R-R-U-N-M-A":

C—Call to order.
R—Read the minutes of the last meeting.
R—Reports of standing committees.
R—Reports of special committees.
U—Unfinished business.

N—New business.
M—Miscellaneous: announcements, requests, etc.
A—Adjournment.

The remarks a chairman commonly has to make while he takes his group through the order of business seem obvious, though they are often mishandled. The following is an essential but not exhaustive list:

1. "The meeting will come to order."
2. "The secretary will read the minutes."
3. "Are there any corrections or additions to the minutes?"
4. "The chair recognizes Mr. Dozier." Or simply, "Mr. Dozier."
5. "Would you put that in the form of a motion?" Or, "Is there a motion that . . . ?"
6. "It has been moved that. . . . Is there a second?"
7. "It has been moved and seconded that. . . . Is there any discussion?"
8. "Any further discussion?"
9. "If there are no objections (pause), we will put the question to a vote. All in favor, say 'Aye.' All opposed, 'No.' The 'ayes' have it. The motion is passed." Where possible, the chairman should guide the assembly to a unanimous vote by saying, "Is there a motion that this proposal be approved (disapproved) by acclamation?"
10. Whenever "suggestions" are made, the chairman should say, "May we have that in the form of a motion?"
11. If a member makes an improper motion, the chairman should suggest the proper one, or more effective wording, rather than ruling the member out of order. The latter action is always available, of course.
12. Any unclear points should be clarified immediately and necessary definitions provided.
13. In summation, the chairman must provide the meeting with technical assistance, indexing devices, and helpful supporting material.
14. The meeting is ended by saying, "Is there a motion to adjourn?"

INTRODUCTIONS

Probably for several more years you will be more apt to *introduce* a speaker than to *be* the speaker. Of all the speeches of courtesy, none may seem so unnecessary as the introduction. After all, the audience usually knows the speaker, knows what he is to speak about, and wants mainly to get on with the show. Yet in fact no courtesy speech is so prevalent.

Your task when you introduce a speaker is to celebrate the audience's feelings about the occasion. You seek to bring audience and speaker closer together. The first thing to remember is that you, the introducer, are relatively unimportant. The second thing is, be brief and to the point. Third and last is, be spontaneous, sincere, and good-humored.

Your proposition will be either "We should listen closely to Mr. X," or "Mr. X is worth listening to," but probably you will conceal the proposal. Obviously one of these propositions focuses on the audience, the other on the speaker. Your points to be amplified will vary to some extent, but they may include the following: (1) the name of the speaker (the only mandatory point); (2) the speaker's accomplishments; (3) the speaker's subject; (4) a description of the audience; (5) a description of the occasion, and in particular how it combines speaker, audience, and subject. Amplification materials should focus on incidents and experiences, rather than descriptions of them. Information is a key support, but it should appear in anecdote or detailed illustration.

Of course, sometimes the occasion itself will sharply limit what you may say in your introduction. The standard introduction from public affairs—"Ladies and gentlemen, the President of the United States"—may fit many less prominent occasions. Another example of propriety (and brevity) comes from Marc Connelly's *The Green Pastures,* Act I, when the Angel Gabriel steps downstage and says, "Gangway! Gangway for de Lawd God Jehovah!" What else need be said?

On the whole, however, your introductions will run longer and contain more details than these two examples. The sample which follows is longer than many introductions because it deliberately includes all possible points. Ordinarily you would seldom use every point developed here, but would strive for greater brevity.

GENERAL PURPOSE: To persuade.

SPECIFIC PURPOSE: To introduce Snoopy to my speech class, Thursday morning, January 5, 1967.

PROPOSITION: Snoopy is worthy of your attention.

TITLE: "Ace of Aces"

TECHNICAL PLOT (What the speaker does)	OUTLINE (What the speaker says)
ATTENTION STEP	Ladies and Gentlemen:
ORIENTATION STEP Authority	As we all know, the twentieth has been the bloodiest of centuries. We're struggling with and through what Winston Churchill called "The Second Thirty Years' War"—only it looks more like fifty or a hundred years from where we sit. You and I have been, are, or soon will be in the front lines of this war.
Quotation	
Identification	
Allusion	The battlefield we fight on is everywhere.
Allusion	We are all Tudors now, and our enemies are the people who created or who perpetuate the mess we live with.

EXPOSITION STEP	Fighting these "adults" is the sworn duty of every
Main Point I	member of our *"Four F Club—*Find 'em, Fake 'em out, Fix 'em, and Fade away."
Main Point II	This morning we've gathered together to inaugurate our first major campaign against the City Fathers.
Main Point III	Here to start us off is the one person we admire.
Sub-Point A	Our speaker this morning has led the fight
Allusion	against our enemies. He has been broken but not defeated. He has shown us how to join up with
Sub-Point B	the world, but still remain our own masters.
PERORATION STEP	Ladies and gentlemen,
	The scourge *and* the victim of the Red Baron— our candidate for President—
	Snoopy!

PRESENTATIONS AND ACCEPTANCES

Once again we examine a kind of speech you will probably have several occasions to make. No doubt you will be receiving more awards than you give for the next few years, but the two speeches are so similar we can study them together.

*The Presentation Speech—*Your job if you present the award is to celebrate the recipient's qualification for it, the value of the award itself, and the audience's part in the award. Again it is important to remember that you are not the star of the occasion. Again you should strive for brevity and complete appropriateness. Again you should be spontaneous, sincere, and good-humored.

Your proposition will be either "We have chosen the right person for our award" or "Mr. X is worthy of this award." Your points to be amplified may vary to some extent, but certainly the most important is the name of the recipient. Close to it in value is the name or the significance of the award. More than these you do not have to celebrate, but many such speeches review the accomplishments or exploits of the recipient, appraise the material and spiritual value of the award, and compliment the losers for a "race well run."

The following example speaks for itself:

GENERAL PURPOSE:	To persuade.
SPECIFIC PURPOSE:	To celebrate the presentation of the Distinguished Service Medal to Lt. Col. John H. Glenn, Jr., February 23, 1962, at Cape Canaveral, Florida [now Cape Kennedy].

PROPOSITION: The American people have chosen wisely in their de-
                        cision to trust and to reward Colonel Glenn.

TITLE: "Presenting the Distinguished Service Medal"*

TECHNICAL PLOT (What the speaker does)	OUTLINE (What the speaker says)
ATTENTION STEP Allusion	Colonel Glenn, will you step forward. Seventeen years ago today, a group of Marines put the American Flag on Mount Suribachi, so it is very
ORIENTATION STEP	appropriate that today we decorate Colonel Glenn of the United States Marine Corps, and
Association Allusion	also realize that in the not too distant future a Marine or a Naval man or an Air Force man will put the American Flag on the moon.
ARGUMENTATION STEP Main Point I Description Information	I present this Citation. The President of the United States takes pleasure in awarding the National Aeronautics and Space Administration's Distinguished Service Medal to Lieutenant Colonel John H. Glenn, Jr., United States Marine Corps, for services set forth in the following: For exceptionally meritorious service to the government of the United States in a duty of great responsibility as the first American astronaut to perform orbital flight. Lieutenant Colonel Glenn's orbital flight on February 20, 1962, made an outstanding contribution to the advancement of human knowledge of space technology and in demonstration of man's capabilities in space flight.
Main Point II	His performance was marked by his great professional knowledge, his skill as a test pilot, his unflinching courage, and his extraordinary ability to perform most difficult tasks under conditions of great physical stress and personal danger. His performance in fulfillment of this most dangerous assignment reflects the highest credit upon himself and the United States.
PERORATION STEP	Colonel, we appreciate what you have done!
	We have Mr. and Mrs. Glenn, who launched Colonel Glenn originally—they are right here in the front row—and also Mrs. Glenn and David and Lynn.
	And we would like to have you say a word to everybody.

The Acceptance Speech—It may seem to you that the acceptance of an award would be easy and simple to make. And it is certainly true that all you really have to say is "Thank you." But usually, if you have no warning, you will find yourself lucky to stammer out that much.

If you have time to prepare in some detail, however, you ought to do more than give thanks. In this instance you are the main attraction. Yet it still behooves you to be brief, spontaneous, sincere, and good-humored. Your task is to celebrate the occasion, not yourself; your team rather than your lonely effort. In the space age as never before, all of us are part of a single family. As President Kennedy's allusion indicates, the most "self-made man" is still the product of a team effort. More than likely, whatever your triumph, literally hundreds or even thousands of people contributed to your success. You the recipient of the award become therefore the representative of these unnamed thousands.

Your proposition thus becomes something like "This award was won by all who helped me become what I am, and we appreciate your generosity." Your main points are the gratitude, the team effort, the gift itself, the spirit of the giver, and the method by which the award was earned. The sample which follows is a classic of its kind.

GENERAL PURPOSE: To persuade.

SPECIFIC PURPOSE: To celebrate the participation of the entire country in Colonel Glenn's achievement and in the award.

PROPOSITION: This award belongs to all the Americans who have struggled to develop a space program.

TITLE: "Accepting the Distinguished Service Medal"*

TECHNICAL PLOT (What the speaker does)	OUTLINE (What the speaker says)
ATTENTION STEP	All right—fine, thank you. Sit down, please—it's hot.
ORIENTATION STEP Allusion Formal Proposition	I can't express my appreciation adequately, to be here accepting this, when I know how many thousands of people all over the country were involved in helping accomplish what we did last Tuesday—and knowing how, particularly this group here at the Cape, and many of the group here on the platform, our own group of astronauts who were scattered all around the world who performed their functions here at the Cape also—we all acted literally and figuratively as a team. It was a real team effort all the way.

*Reprinted from *Principles of Speech*, 5th brief ed., by Alan H. Monroe and Douglas Ehninger. Copyright © 1964 by Scott, Foresman and Company.

ARGUMENTATION STEP	We have stressed the team effort in Project Mercury. It goes across the board—I think sort of a cross-cut of Americana, of industry, and military, and Civil Service—government work—contractors. It's almost a cross-cut of American effort in the technical field—I think it wasn't specialized by any one particular group. It was headed up by NASA, of course, but thousands and thousands of people have contributed, certainly as much or more than I have to the Project.
Main Point I	
Explanation	
Main Point II	
Explanation	
SUMMATION STEP	I would like to consider that I was sort of a figure-head for the whole big, tremendous effort. And I am very proud of the Medal I have on my lapel here, for all of us—you included—because I think it represents all of our efforts—not just mine. Thank you very much. And thank you, Mr. President.
PERORATION STEP	

WELCOMES AND RESPONSES

You may feel that you will not soon do anything worthy of a medal. Yet probably you have already joined many a group. Perhaps you have not been formally welcomed, or have not had to conduct the acknowledgment of someone else's membership, but if you remain in the group that time will surely come.

The Speech of Welcome.—The leader of a group, or his representative, normally has the job of saying with tact and good feeling, "We're glad you're here." This straightforward statement serves well as the proposition of a "speech of welcome." The points to be amplified are (1) the reason the person is visiting or is present with the group; (2) the group's accomplishments or history; (3) the reason for the welcome, if it is a special one; and (4) prediction of happy or successful times now that the visitor or new member is with the group. As in all speeches of courtesy, it is necessary to be spontaneous, sincere, and brief. The following sample was designed for an imaginary situation, but it involves a real place and actual people.

GENERAL PURPOSE:	To persuade.
SPECIFIC PURPOSE:	To welcome Dr. Gifford Wingate as new Chairman of the Drama and Speech Department at Texas Western College, on the occasion of the Annual Debate Banquet.
PROPOSITION:	We are glad you are here.
TITLE:	"Howdy, Pardner."

TECHNICAL PLOT (What the speaker does)	OUTLINE (What the speaker says)
ATTENTION STEP	Ladies and gentlemen:
ORIENTATION STEP	At debate banquets we come to see who got the hardware and which judge did what to whom, and to have a free meal before we hear the good or bad news.
Authentication	As coach of the Texas Western Debate Squad, it's my privilege to welcome you to this Seventh Annual Sun Carnival Debate Tournament. Your cooperation and good fellowship as we stumbled through the new construction to our rooms, as we struggled with schedules thrown awry by the distances you had to travel to be here, and as the usual foul-ups were held to a normal minimum, well, let's just say you made the tournament a success, not me.
Allusion	
Allusion	
Identification	
ARGUMENTATION STEP Main Point I	This is an especially momentous occasion, as many of you know. It's the first Sun Carnival Tournament for our new chairman, Dr. Gifford Wingate.
Information	
Topic Sentence	I'd better add his name to yours as one of the people responsible for the success of the tournament.
Main Point II Topic Sentence	Dr. Wingate arrived at Texas Western only last September. Already he has given our department a new sense of direction, of going somewhere, indeed of achievement.
Information Illustration	He has instituted a master's program in speech —with a minor in drama—and laid the groundwork for a doctor's program in one or two years.
Information Illustration	Earlier this evening he told me that at the SAA convention he bid in three Ph.D.'s—two in speech and one in drama. One of the speech men is
Explanation	a nationally-known therapist, so that program should get off the ground soon, too.
Restatement Information	This semester—his first here—he has personally directed two plays and has led the theatre staff in revitalizing the drama program.
SUMMATION STEP	As you can see, those of us in speech, speech therapy, and drama—the whole field—have reason to welcome Gif Wingate.
PERORATION STEP	We're glad he's here, and we're sure that all of us in the Trans-Pecos Region say, "Howdy, pardner!"

The Response to a Welcome.—Like the speech acknowledging an award, the response to a welcome often consists only of "Thank you." With this phrase alone you can succeed, and no matter what else you add, if this thought is missing, your speech will probably fail.

Yet if you have the chance to compose your thoughts, you may want to do more than give thanks. Your proposition in this case should be "I am glad to be here" or "I appreciate this welcome." Among the points to be amplified are (1) the significance of the occasion, (2) your personal involvement with the group, (3) the achievements of the group, (4) the contributions of others to your accomplishments, and (5) the prediction of happy experiences. The following sample continues the imaginary situation we have just examined.

GENERAL PURPOSE: To persuade.

SPECIFIC PURPOSE: To respond to the welcome extended by the Debate Coach at the Debate Banquet.

PROPOSITION: I am glad to be a part of Texas Western's growing Drama and Speech Department.

TITLE: "Miner by Choice"

TECHNICAL PLOT (What the speaker does)	(OUTLINE) (What the speaker says)
ATTENTION STEP	Thank you, Gene.
ORIENTATION STEP	And thank you, everyone. Excuse me. I mean "you all."
ARGUMENTATION STEP Main Point I Allusion Topic Sentence	As one of the judges of this tournament, I must hasten to point out a basic contradiction in Gene's case. On the one hand, the savior, Gifford Wingate, is welcomed. On the other, the welcome is extended at the *seventh* annual Sun Carnival Tournament. Seems to me the saving occurred long before I got here.
Main Point II Identification Authentication Topic Sentence	Not that I deny the accomplishments Gene told you about. I'm proud of our record this past semester. We all are. And we have a right to be, for we all helped push the new programs through. My name is signed to the letters, but the whole department wrote what's in them.
Main Point III Identification Allusion Rhetorical Question	And finally, how many of you, like me, are Texans—or Southwesterners—by choice. Raise your hands. You see? More than half. No wonder the Trans-Pecos is growing so fast. Do any of you regret for one moment tearing up your roots in the East or the North or the Midwest and coming here? We face many problems and challenges

Allusion	over the next few years. But I doubt we would trade this atmosphere of enthusiasm and vigor for the tired, problem-less one we left behind.
Topic Sentence	I know I wouldn't.
SUMMATION STEP	So what I have received by way of a new scope for experimentation, new ideas, and bold programs, in the midst of a department well on its way to greatness, far outweighs what I have brought to Texas Western.
PERORATION STEP	I stand taller now, and it's not just my new Tony Lama boots.
	It's my new life: I'm a Southwesterner, I'm a Texan, I'm a Miner by choice.

THE GOODWILL SPEECH

It has been stated that goodwill speeches play a major role in the public relations activities of many business firms and other institutions. Perhaps it is so. Recently, at the opening session of a professional convention that I attended, two-thirds of the speeches ostensibly reporting on the work of various offices in the organizations holding the convention did in fact seem more concerned about reinforcing favorable attitudes than delivering information.

In the goodwill speech you may provide information and explanation, but your specific purpose is to reinforce or develop affirmative attitudes toward the organization you represent. Thus, if you have been asked to bring information or to demonstrate an activity or a product, your points and their supports are controlled not by the subject matter itself, but by its persuasive effect on your audience. Your proposition should be either fact or value: "X Corporation serves your interests" or "X Corporation is worthy of respect for its public-spirited policies." Ordinarily the materials used to amplify your topic should be wholly germane to the announced subject. Straightforward information, as we have noted, is often the best kind of persuasion. But if the subject as a whole is not suitable to the securing of goodwill, you must select those parts of the subject that do fit your purpose. Your points in exposition usually will be something like (1) the relationship of the subject to the audience, where this is affirmative; (2) new facts about the subject; (3) the "public service" aspects of the subject; (4) definite services available to the audience; and (5) amazing aspects of the subject. The following speech was prepared as an example of the goodwill address for this textbook. Although most of the names have been changed, the situation actually occurred over a period of several months in the life of the author. That is, a number of meetings have been coalesced into a single occasion.

GENERAL PURPOSE: To persuade.

SPECIFIC PURPOSE: To reinforce favorable attitudes toward the University Theatre.

PROPOSITION: Your University Theatre deserves your full support.

TITLE: "Theatre Begins with Wonder"

TECHNICAL PLOT (What the speaker does)	OUTLINE (What the speaker says)
ATTENTION STEP Allusion	Thank you, Mrs. Jeffords. And my thanks to all of you for this pleasant luncheon. If I'm half the man described in the introduction you just heard, I may well quit while I'm ahead.
ORIENTATION STEP Identification Association Authentication Identification Right to Speak Identification	But now that I'm a Flying Miner, nothing can stop me from moving down the field. I hope the expression on my face reveals just how happy I am to be in El Paso, at the University of Texas, working in the educational theatre that we all love. It's been too many years since I breathed good Texas air. My first impression of El Paso is that it's just like Dallas, where I was raised, only more beautiful. John Carpenter has told me how exciting the relationship between your Association for Children's Theatre and the University Theatre has been. Naturally I'd like that excitement about our programs to continue. So often, with a new regime, come changes in goals, in methods, and in spirit. With the advent of so many new professors of drama from Cornell (my own school), Ohio State, and our own U.T., it's likely you have a good many questions about the state of the drama program at your own university on the mountain.
Formal Purpose	This afternoon I'd like to explain your university theatre program.
Formal Partition	First I'd like to show you how the overall program works for you—what we have in store for our general audiences of students, teachers like yourselves and our own faculty, and other citizens of the El Paso Southwest, who've so generously supported our efforts in the past. Then I'd like to tell you about our plans for children's theatre.
(Transition)	(Let's begin therefore with an examination of our "living library of theatre.")

ARGUMENTATION STEP
Identification

In our national pursuit of higher education, we Americans often forget that attending a university is first of all an *experience*. More important than what a person learns is what he *becomes*. While his body and brain will age at least four years during his life as a college student, his mind and soul ought to grow several centuries as a result of his immersion in the ideas and feelings propounded by five thousand years of civilization. To that end, primarily, universities hire professors, build laboratories, and fill libraries.

Rationalization

Formal Main Point I

To that end, also, the Department of Drama and Speech at The University of Texas at El Paso (*your* university) has joined with the University Players to establish a "living library of theatre." Their goal is to provide during a student's four-year matriculation at least one play from each period of human history from which we have dramatic works. During the next four years, for example, we plan to show the following:

Sub-Point A

Illustration

1. This year:
   a. Ancient Greece: *Oedipus the King*.
   b. Eighteenth-Century England: *The Beggar's Opera*.
   c. Twentieth-Century America: *A Thousand Clowns*.
   d. Medieval England: *The Second Shepherd's Play* and *Everyman*.
2. Next year:
   a. Seventeenth-Century France: *The Miser*.
   b. Jacobean England: *The Alchemist*.
   c. Twentieth-Century France: *The Balcony*.
   d. Nineteenth-Century England: *The Importance of Being Earnest*.
3. 1969-70:
   a. Elizabethan England: *Dr. Faustus*.
   b. Nineteenth-Century America: *Fashion*.
   c. Seventeenth-Century England: *The Country Wife*.
   d. Nineteenth-Century Norway: *Hedda Gabler*.
4. 1970-71:
   a. Elizabethan England: *King Lear*.
   b. Ancient Greece: *Medea*
   c. Twentieth-Century America: *Desire Under the Elms*.
   d. Twentieth-Century Italy: *The Queen and the Rebels*.

Sub-Point B	During each of these seasons we plan to offer an original musical. We hope that playwrights and composers will submit musical plays that accurately portray the shifting values of our time, but that affirm the worth of life and the triumph
Illustration	of the human spirit. Like *West Side Story* or *Cabaret*, for example. What we expect to create
Sub-Point C	in both the plays and the musicals is the form and spirit of an era, seen through the eyes of a
Sub-Point D	dramatist typical of the era. Seeing a total world presented on stage, the student will expand his own vision to that of the playwright, and will achieve something like the poet's understanding of the ideas and feelings examined in the play.
Sub-Point E (Argument I)	No other university experience offers the student so complete a participation in the life and times of the culture that defines his humanity.
(Transition)	(But not only the students in the audience gain from the living library. What about the students on stage and back stage?)
Sub-Point F (Argument II)	Those students who help create the productions can reach even greater intimacy with the minds of great poets and artists. Only a few of these
Information	actors and technicians plan to earn their living after college with their theatre skills. The great
Explanation Allusion	majority work in the theatre because they find their university lives expanded the furthest when they themselves reveal to their age its form and pressure. They experience by doing, they learn by becoming, and they become by learning.
(Transition)	(Thus far I've talked only of "students." What about the rest of El Paso?)
Sub-Point G Allusion	Well, in the first place, you and I who are teachers know better than most how important it is for all of us to remain "students" of the world and all that dwell therein. In the second place, to answer my question more directly, I can assure you that the living library of theatre is conscious of, and will carry out the university's responsi-
(Argument III)	bility to this community. For you as well as for the students who are formally enrolled, the University Players seek to prepare a vision of your times both past and present.
(Internal Summary)	(To all of El Paso, to the entire student body, therefore, the Players address themselves: "On your imaginary forces let us work, and with your thoughts come deck our kings. Let us give you truth in the pleasant guise of illusion. There can

be no richer life than that lived in your own university theatre.")

(Transition)

(Besides offering you the living library of theater, your university plans to enlarge and expand its program of children's plays.)

Formal Main Point II

The Department of Drama and Speech, in association with the University Players, is proud to announce the American Children's Theatre Institute. The department plans to combine our courses in creative dramatics with a touring company that will present one play each semester in the schools around the city and a third play

Sub-Point A

in Magoffin Auditorium during February. This fall we will offer *Alice in Wonderland*. In the

Sub-Point B

spring we will tour *Huckleberry Finn*. The week of February 19-24, we will produce *Winnie-the-*

Identification

Pooh in Magoffin. This play is the production for which you have contracted to bring the children from all the schools. Your support of our annual children's play for ten years now has brought over 75,000 children to the campus. We'd like your help in expanding this program to include the fall and spring tours—so that three

(Argument IV)

times as many children can experience the wonder of theater. We believe our new institute can best succeed if your association manages the performance dates, the audiences in the schools

Illustration

where you teach, and the ticket sales, just as you now do for the single production in Magof-

Explanation

fin. Naturally we'd like to use the same financial arrangement that's served us so well for the past

Identification

ten years.

SUMMATION STEP

In fact, because our interests seem so closely linked, I have brought you this blueprint for the future. Theatre is experience of the life and times we all live in. Theatre is creation of the form and pressure of each and all the worlds men have made for themselves. But most of all, theatre is a way to expand our view of life. For theatre begins with wonder—the wonder of a child.

PERORATION STEP

So I bring you a plea for the future. For both parts of our theatre program—the living library *and* the theatre of wonder—as audience *and* as participant—on your imaginations let us work, and with your thoughts come deck our kings. Theatre begins with wonder, but it ends with enlightenment. Between these two moments lie much toil and travail. Let us join together to

work and give, so that our theatre may live.
There can be no richer life than that spent in
your own university theatre.

SUGGESTIONS FOR FURTHER READINGS

BRIGANCE, W. N. *Speech: Its Techniques and Disciplines in a Free Society.*
2nd ed. New York: Appleton-Century-Crofts, Inc., 1961. Chapter XXIII.
BRYANT, DONALD C., and KARL R. WALLACE. *Oral Communication: A Short
Course in Speaking.* 3rd ed. New York: Appleton-Century-Crofts, Inc.,
1962. Chapter XIV.
MONROE, ALAN H., and DOUGLAS EHNINGER. *Principles of Speech.* 5th brief
ed. Chicago: Scott, Foresman and Co., 1964. Chapter XI.
McBURNEY, J. H. and E. J. WRAGE. *The Art of Good Speech.* New York:
Prentice-Hall, Inc., 1955. Chapter XXV.

Chapter 5

SPEECHES OF
COMMEMORATION

Human beings seldom bury their dead, retire from a position, begin a new venture, or celebrate an anniversary without "saying a few words." Using the audience's dominant attitudes (whether active or latent), the speaker magnifies or minifies a person, a place, or an experience. Explanation and courtesy techniques (see Chapters 3 and 4) are combined to amplify a proposition of value regarding the subject of the address. The past is developed in concrete and specific ways; the future, only in a general way.

The four commemorative speeches are the eulogy, the farewell, the dedication, and the anniversary. A speech that combined three of these four was President Lyndon Johnson's Thanksgiving Address to the Congress in November, 1963, following the assassination of John F. Kennedy. The president eulogized Kennedy, bid him farewell, and dedicated himself to furthering the goals of the Kennedy Administration. The proposition—"Let us continue"—allowed for an almost perfect fusion of audience attitudes and beliefs with Johnson's recommendations about past, present, and future. Whether commemoration was only a tool of Johnson's persuasion or whether he merely adapted perfectly to the situation is certainly debatable. But audience and occasion *required* a speech very much like the one Johnson provided.

THE EULOGY

In this speech you develop in some detail the ideas your audience holds about your subject, and strive to crystallize the sentiments to which these ideas are anchored. Although you must deal with your subject's primary qualities, you are most concerned with the people in your audience. You celebrate their peculiar relationship with the person or place being magnified or minified. Supports are chosen first for their effect, second for their actual importance in the life of the subject. You may praise or blame, cover an entire life or only parts of it, so long as you phrase accurately what your audience is feeling.

A classic proposition for this kind of speech might be Hamlet's "He was a man, take him for all in all" or Antony's "This was the noblest Roman of them all." Your supports, mainly informational, should focus on (1) the central purpose of your subject's life or history; (2) the qualities that made your subject what he or it was; (3) the incidents that endeared your subject to your audience; (4) the reason for whatever impact he or it had; and (5) the lesson to be learned from the life or history.

The following speech eulogizes an actual person who was killed in the crash of an air force tanker, although the precise speech situation never occurred.

GENERAL PURPOSE: To persuade.

SPECIFIC PURPOSE: To celebrate the life of First Lieutenant Richard Corey King (KIA 25 June 1956).

PROPOSITION: Richard Corey King epitomized our generation of "professional civilian soldiers."

TITLE: "Go On and Prosper"

TECHNICAL PLOT (What the speaker does)	OUTLINE (What the speaker says)
ATTENTION STEP Allusion	In the days when we were flying missions over the roof of the world, our final contact with civilization came when we coasted out into the empty stillness of the Arctic sky. That last contact was our final radar check, and always the controller helped us on our way. "Cherio!" the operator cried. "Cherio, yank! Go on and prosper!"
Quotation	
IDENTIFICATION STEP Main Point I Information	Richard Corey King was my airplane commander, my pilot, and my friend. With him for over a year I flew three times a week on every kind of mission there was. To him on more than one occasion I owed the only life I had. For him on every flight I gladly risked that life.
Allusion Allusion Information Allusion	For all of you who shared our loneliness, or who waited for us, I needn't beautify the record. You know that Richard never failed a mission or missed a rendezvous—even when the widowmakers sent us off beyond our safest weight and human tolerance. You know we called him "Sky King" because of his success and punctuality—a nickname started in derision but continued in

Information

Main Point II

Main Point III

Allusion

Formal Proposition

Allusion

Association

Main Point IV
Allusion

Association

Information

Allusion
Information

Main Point V

Main Point VI

Allusion

gratitude by the bomber pilots running out of fuel. On the day Richard's crew had the duty, *all* the bombers made it safely home. Whatever the mission, wherever the rendezvous, however we had to violate the law of averages and the laws of physics, Sky King made it easy for us. When even birds were scared to fly, his courage and his skill would keep us going.

And even in the face of odds that turned to worse instead of better, Richard never sought the easy pick-me-up of patriotism offered by the men with stars and the fat and happy people that we flew for. There was never any need for heroics. The American people paid for our missions, and with Sky King in the lead, they got more than market value for their money. Richard was a true professional—a man who added up the score, counted up the odds, and played the game with everything he had. Like all the men who keep us from the edge of darkness, he counted it a privilege to carry out our orders with perfection.

And those of us who lost this key to grace dropped out along the way. Those of us who let the actions of the people we were flying for blind us to the end we sought threw away our skill, and left the job to those who hadn't lost the way. That I am here before you marks my failure. That my experience and skill might have made the difference to the man the touch of death had made my brother—that I and I alone might have helped him to return alive just one more time—this thought will haunt me throughout all my life.

For on a day last week when you and I were basking in the sun, and Dick was taking off into the empty heat of a New Mexico afternoon, the violated laws of physics claimed their justice. In a plane overloaded "By Order of the Commander," Sky King returned to earth in a flaming shower of metal. There beside a lonely road— with all his crew but still without heroics—died a man who was carrying out a mission we had started with our fancy rhetoric, and had failed to finish in our shameful fear.

Those of us who love our safety bought the lives of Dick and all his crew with some extra bucks a month, and a shining silver airplane that makes a man a god if given half a chance. We threw

away their fineness and their strength as if we
owned them because no one else would take the
job. In all our years to come we will walk in
health and happiness because they were glad to
offer theirs for ours.

Main Point VII

To capture what they did we have no words.
The trade-school cry of "Honor, God, and Country!" mocks the deed that called it forth. Rich-

Allusion

ard wasn't a clean-limbed, crew-cut boy filled
with dead and empty glories of a past more lied

Allusion

about than loved. He was simply a guy who said,
"If Uncle Sugar wants a man, let him take me."

Peroration Step

For all of them, for all the men who spend their
courage and their skill to keep us resting easy
in our beds, who stand between us and the darkness—for each of them, and for this man—for
this *man*—who was my friend, I cry in anguish
to the empty afternoon: "Cherio! Cherio, Sky
King! Go on and prosper!"

THE FAREWELL

This speech is something like a "eulogy of oneself." The same attitudes are celebrated, the same points amplified. To them are added
only (1) reasons for leaving and (2) a prediction of the future in broad
terms. The following speech is probably one of the most famous farewell
addresses that we have.

General Purpose: To persuade.

Specific Purpose: To celebrate Abraham Lincoln's life in Springfield, Illi-
                   nois.

Proposition: To you, my friends, I owe everything.

Title: "Farewell Address"

TECHNICAL PLOT (What the speaker does)	OUTLINE (What the speaker says)
Attention Step	My friends—
Identification Step	No one, not in my situation, can appreciate my feeling of sadness at this parting. To this place, and the kindness of these people, I owe every-
Information	thing. Here I have lived a quarter of a century, and have passed from a young to an old man.
Information	Here my children have been born, and one is
Information	buried. I now leave, not knowing when, or
Association	whether ever, I may return, with a task before me greater than that which rested upon Wash-

PERORATION STEP

ington. Without the assistance of that Divine Being, who ever attended him, I cannot succeed. With that assistance I cannot fail. Trusting in Him, who can go with me, and remain with you and be everywhere for good, let us confidently hope that all will yet be well. To His care commending you, as I hope in your prayers you will commend me, I bid you an affectionate farewell.

THE DEDICATION

Not only the passing of a man, or his departure. from a place, but also the instituting of something new calls for a special speech. The purpose is to celebrate the meaning of the new building, memorial, or organization. The proposition is something like "This building should inspire us to carry out the tasks which it symbolizes." The points for amplification usually are (1) the reasons for the construction; (2) the costs in blood and treasure; (3) the qualities of the builders; (4) the value of the construction; and (5) the specific tasks which the structure or institution should inspire us to accomplish.

GENERAL PURPOSE: To persuade.

SPECIFIC PURPOSE: To celebrate the national significance of the new cemetery at Gettysburg.

PROPOSITION: The sacrifice represented by the cemetery at Gettysburg should cause increased devotion to freedom in the United States.

TITLE: "Address at Gettysburg"

TECHNICAL PLOT (What the speaker does)	OUTLINE (What the speaker says)
ATTENTION STEP	Four score and seven years ago our fathers brought forth on this continent, a new nation, conceived in liberty, and dedicated to the proposition that all men are created equal.
IDENTIFICATION STEP	Now we are engaged in a great civil war, testing whether that nation, or any nation so conceived and so dedicated, can long endure. We are met on a great battlefield of that war. We have come to dedicate a portion of that field, as a final resting place for those who here gave their lives that that nation might live. It is altogether fitting and proper that we should do this.
Main Point I	
Main Point II	But, in a larger sense, we cannot dedicate— we cannot consecrate—we cannot hallow—this ground. The brave men, living and dead, who

Formal Proposition

struggled here, have consecrated it, far above our poor power to add or detract. The world will little note, nor long remember what we say here, but it can never forget what they did here. It is for us the living, rather, to be dedicated here to the unfinished work which they who fought here have thus far so nobly advanced. It is rather for us to be here dedicated to the great task remaining before us—that from these honored dead we take increased devotion—that we here highly resolve that these dead shall not have died in vain—that this nation, under God, shall have a new birth of freedom—and that government of the people, by the people, for the people, shall not perish from the earth.

PERORATION STEP

THE ANNIVERSARY SPEECH

In this commemorative address a holiday of some kind is celebrated. July Fourth, Labor Day, Memorial Day, even Christmas—these and others symbolize a moment of high truth in American or Western culture. Thus the anniversary speech celebrates the event or the action that the holiday commemorates. Its significance for the present audience is amplified. The proposition for a Memorial Day speech, to take one example, might be "This day means 'freedom' to a people still struggling for it." The points to be amplified may include (1) details of the event being celebrated; (2) the ideals and values inherent in the event; (3) the effect or influence of the event; and (4) the lessons to be learned from it.

The sample speech given below was composed for an imaginary holiday—Constitution Day, the one hundred and eightieth anniversary of the adoption of the Constitution of the United States of America, September 17, 1787.

GENERAL PURPOSE: To persuade.

SPECIFIC PURPOSE: To celebrate Constitution Day, September 17, 1967.

PROPOSITION: We should support and defend the Constitution with our lives, our fortunes, and our sacred honor.

TITLE: "The Constitution, Right or Wrong!"

TECHNICAL PLOT (What the speaker does)	OUTLINE (What the speaker says)
ATTENTION STEP	Mr. President, Fellow Teachers and Parents, Ladies and Gentlemen:
IDENTIFICATION STEP	When we opened this meeting we stood together and recited the Pledge of Allegiance to the Flag

Right to Speak

Allusion

Right to Speak

Allusion

Association

Restatement

Explanation

Allusion

Quotation

Explanation
Allusion

Allusion

Allusion
Quotation

Explanation

of the United States of America. Such is the practice at every PTA meeting I have ever attended. Such is the practice in our classrooms and in our assemblies. When the flag comes by us as we watch a parade, we stand and remove our hats; if we are in uniform, we salute. Out at the university where I teach, all traffic stops when the flag is lowered each day at five in the afternoon. On each of these occasions we hear grumbling. The few seconds it takes to render respect to our flag is begrudged by many Americans. Well, I have felt that way too from time to time.

But surely none of us who grumble can fail to realize that it is not the flag we salute, but the country. It is not the "Grand Old Rag," as George M. Cohan lovingly called it, but the grand old republic that we honor when we pledge allegiance. It is not the flag we defend throughout the world, but the country.

And when we say "country" we don't mean only the real estate. We don't mean only the sharply smoky New England autumn; the lush colors along the Azalea Trail in South Carolina; the vast prairies of the Midwest; the stark and savage desert from here to California; the overwhelming grandeur of the Rockies, the Sierra Nevadas, and the Grand Tetons; the promise of the Pacific Northwest; or the brawling, sprawling cities of steel and stone across the land. No, we don't mean only these when we say, "My country, may she always be in the right, but my country, right or wrong."

Nor do we mean only the life that Nathan Hale gave with the regret that it was all he had. Nor do we mean only the band of brothers who felt it necessary and proper to give their lives for ours: Private Edwin Jennison, from a truly lost generation, killed at Malvern Hill, and all the unnamed dead at The Wilderness with Grant, "where even boys counted"; Sergeant York, and the Lost Battalion; Audie Murphy, and Rodger Young; all the young men, black, white, brown, yellow, whose blood runs together in the soil around Saigon and the Chongjin Reservoir. "God send me to see suche a company together agayne when need is." [Lord Howard of Effingham]

Nor do we mean only the great men who belong to the ages: Washington and Jefferson and Benjamin Franklin; Lincoln and Robert E. Lee; the Roosevelts and Wendell Wilkie; and General Sam Houston.

(Transition)

All these are our country, but they have days enough to honor them. Today is Sunday, September 17, 1967. We are gathered for a picnic celebrating the start of our new school year. One hundred and eighty years ago from this date, a group of men gathered to celebrate adoption of a document they had written. Some years before,

Allusion

they had pledged their lives, their fortunes, and their sacred honor to the cause of independence. At that time they had said they held "these truths to be self-evident, that all men are created equal; that they are endowed by their Creator

Quotation

with certain unalienable rights; that among these are life, liberty, and the pursuit of happiness." After a terrible war, these men gathered again. They wanted to test their belief that governments are instituted among men to secure the

Allusion

rights proclaimed in the Declaration of Independence.

Now these lawyers, farmers, businessmen, and teachers wrote a document that began: "We the

Quotation

people of the United States, in order to form a more perfect union, establish justice, insure domestic tranquility, provide for the common defense, promote the general welfare, and secure the blessings of liberty to ourselves and our posterity, do ordain and establish this Constitution of the United States of America."

Restatement

Today, September 17, 1967, is the anniversary of the ratification of that Constitution. Good men in Maine and Texas, in California and Florida—Americans all—should celebrate this anniversary like they do none other. For nothing is so much our country as our Constitution. Without it, lit-

Formal Proposition

erally, there can be no United States of America —at least none that I would want to live in.

(Transition)

I am sure you understand my feelings.

RATIONALIZATION STEP

Main Point I

Without going into great detail, cannot we all agree that government should rest on a social contract and should have only such powers as

Rhetorical Question

we the people give it? "Popular sovereignty" and "limited government" are the heart of our Constitution.

Main Point II
Rhetorical Question

Cannot we all agree that both the national and the state governments should exercise sovereign power in particular spheres of activity? "Federalism" is the heart of our Constitution.

Main Point III

Cannot we all agree that the government should be one of enumerated powers only? The Tenth Amendment is the heart of our Constitution.

Quotation

You all know what it says: "The powers not delegated to the United States by the Constitution, nor prohibited to it by the States, are reserved to the States respectively, or to the people."

Main Point IV
Rhetorical Question

Cannot we all agree that the national government is supreme in exercising the powers granted to it? If we cannot, then a lot of young men have died in vain.

Main Point V
Rhetorical Question

Authority

Cannot we all agree that there should be a separation of powers among a legislative, an executive, and a judicial branch? Whichever branch we favor at the moment, we need only read our history to see the wisdom of the Founding Fathers. It has not been easy to work with three branches of government, but who among us prefers tyranny to travail?

Main Point VI

Explanation

Cannot we all agree that the judiciary should be supreme? Ah, here we have a controversy! In every generation some people are pro-judicial review, and some people are anti-judicial review. The fact that these people exchange political and economic sides every generation should indicate that the judiciary is the sole bulwark of the people against any arbitrary seizure of power.

Main Point VII
Rhetorical Question

Rhetorical Question

Rhetorical Question

Restatement

Cannot we all agree to accept the Bill of Rights for all our citizens? Should not every American attend the church of his choice, speak his mind when he wants to, and petition the government? Should not every American have the right to assemble peaceably, to live where he wants to, and to keep and bear arms? Should not every American be protected from encroachment by the military, be secure in his home and in his person, and be entitled to legal counsel? Should not every American be entitled to avoid double jeopardy and to have a quick and speedy trial by his peers when he is accused of breaking the law? In short, is there one among us who would deny any American the natural rights and liberties, the civil rights and liberties, that Nathan Hale gave his life so cheerfully to secure and to defend?

Summation Step

Ladies and gentlemen, can there be any doubt that the flag of the United States of America

symbolizes a Constitution which guarantees all of
us—men and women, black, white, yellow, brown,
and red, young and old—a written Constitution,
I say, that on this date is one hundred and eighty
years old—a sacred compact that *guarantees* all
Americans the blessings of life, liberty, and the
pursuit of happiness?

PERORATION STEP   Can there be any doubt, ladies and gentlemen
of the PTA, that on this Constitution Day, the
seventeenth of September, 1967, our country is
our Constitution? Can there be any doubt that
we owe to it our lives, our fortunes, and our
sacred honor? Let us here resolve in all our
thoughts and deeds to give our lives to support
and defend the Constitution of the United States
of America.

SUGGESTIONS FOR FURTHER READING

BAIRD, A. CRAIG, *American Public Addresses 1740-1952.* New York: McGraw-
Hill, 1956.

BRIGANCE, W. N., *Speech: Its Techniques and Disciplines in a Free Society.*
2nd ed. New York: Appleton-Century-Crofts, 1961. Chapter XXIII.

BRYANT, DONALD C., and KARL R. WALLACE. *Oral Communication: A Short
Course in Speaking.* 3rd ed. New York: Appleton-Century-Crofts, 1962.
Chapter XIV.

CAPP, GLENN R., *Famous Speeches in American History.* Indianapolis, Ind.:
Bobbs-Merrill, 1963.

MONROE, ALAN H., and DOUGLAS EHNINGER. *Principles of Speech.* 5th brief
ed. Chicago: Scott, Foresman, 1964.

PARRISH, WAYLAND MAXFIELD, and MARIE HOCHMUTH. *American Speeches.*
New York: Longmans, Green, 1954.

Chapter 6

SPEECHES OF COUNSEL

In Chapter 5 we noted that President Lyndon Johnson's speech of commemoration for John F. Kennedy seemed especially suited to the situation. From this speech onward for about two years, Johnson had an almost unbroken string of executive and legislative successes. He was able to crystallize the surge of emotion about the late president into an effective and practical campaign. The congress was galvanized to pass long-stalled Kennedy proposals. The following autumn, the electorate was driven to give Johnson a landslide at the polls.

The speech in question—in which Johnson identified audience attitudes toward Kennedy with recommendations about future action— seems to have been the initial plea for Johnson's program. Such attempts to counsel in a celebratory situation are not unusual. For a speaker who is an "incumbent" of some kind—that is, representative of an "establishment"—counseling situations make up the major portion of his public speaking.

The point that separates commemoration from counseling is arbitrary. Eulogies, farewells, dedications, and anniversaries can predict the future in a general way: "we should continue" or, more likely, "we should re-establish." The true counseling speech, however, is more specific in its recommendations. The prescription for behavior requires the audience to consider alternative proposals, but they are likely to be *values* rather than *policies*. If there is to be a debate in the mind of the listener, it is to focus on *ends* rather than *means*. The audience is asked to assume a new value-judgment.

THE INAUGURAL ADDRESS

The genius of American politics is the way in which elections are allowed for the moment to settle all issues. No matter how vitriolic the campaign, both losers and winners bend over backwards to heal wounds the election may have dealt the country. Except on rare occasions, therefore, our political offices change hands without the use of force so characteristic of other systems.

The inaugural address traditionally plays a major role in this peaceful turn-over. The victorious president nearly always offers his audience a proposition like Jefferson's "We are all Federalists; we are all Republicans." Each main point amplifies a different group of attitudes. Taken together, the points magnify a sense of unity and minify beliefs that may divide the country. The audience is asked to identify with happy and successful practices from the past, and to work for continuation of these practices in the future.

Lincoln's "Second Inaugural," which follows, sought to heal the wounds of two elections, a vituperative convention, and four years of war.

GENERAL PURPOSE: To persuade.

SPECIFIC PURPOSE: To celebrate the essential unity of the United States of America.

PROPOSITION: All the people of the United States share the guilt for making the war, the depredations of the war, and the responsibility for establishing a just and lasting peace in which all wounds are healed.

TITLE: "Second Inaugural Address*

TECHNICAL PLOT (What the speaker does)	OUTLINE (What the speaker says)
ATTENTION STEP	FELLOW-COUNTRYMEN:
IDENTIFICATION STEP	At this second appearing to take the oath of the presidential office there is less occasion for an extended address than there was at the first. Then a statement somewhat in detail of a course to be pursued seemed fitting and proper. Now, at the expiration of four years, during which public declarations have been constantly called forth on every point and phase of the great contest which still absorbs the attention and engrosses the energies of the nation, little that is new could be presented. The progress of our arms, upon which all else chiefly depends, is as well known to the public as to myself, and it is, I trust, reasonably satisfactory and encouraging
Main Point I	
Association	
Information	
Illustration	
Allusion	

*From *Famous Speeches in American History*, edited by Glenn R. Capp, (Indianapolis, Indiana: The Bobbs-Merrill Company, Inc., 1963), pp. 94, reprinted by permission of the publishers.

to all. With high hope for the future, no prediction in regard to it is ventured.

Main Point II

Association

Association

Association

On the occasion corresponding to this four years ago all thoughts were anxiously directed to an impending civil war. All dreaded it, all sought to avert it. While the inaugural address was being delivered from this place, devoted altogether to *saving* the Union without war, insurgent agents were in the city seeking to *destroy* it without war —seeking to dissolve the Union and divide effects by negotiation. Both parties deprecated war, but one of them would *make* war rather than let the nation survive, and the other would *accept* war rather than let it perish, and the war came.

Information

Allusion

Sub-Point A

Association
Association

Association

Association

Sub-Point B

Allusion

Allusion
Association

Sub-Point C
Quotation

Rhetorical
Question

One-eighth of the whole population was colored slaves, not distributed generally over the Union, but localized in the southern part of it. These slaves constituted a peculiar and powerful interest. All knew that this interest was somehow the cause of the war. To strengthen, perpetuate, and extend this interest was the object for which the insurgents would rend the Union even by war, while the Government claimed no right to do more than to restrict the territorial enlargement of it. Neither party expected for the war the magnitude or the duration which it has already attained. Neither anticipated that the *cause* of the conflict might cease with or even before the conflict itself should cease. Each looked for an easier triumph, and a result less fundamental and astounding. Both read the same Bible and pray to the same God, and each invokes His aid against the other. It may seem strange that any men should dare to ask a just God's assistance in wringing their bread from the sweat of other men's faces, but let us judge not, that we be not judged. The prayers of both could not be answered. That of neither has been answered fully. The Almighty has His own purposes. "Woe unto the world because of offenses; for it must needs be that offenses come, but woe to that man by whom the offense cometh." If we shall suppose that American slavery is one of those offenses which, in the providence of God, must needs come, but which, having continued through His appointed time, He now wills to remove, and that He gives to both North and South this terrible war as the woe due to those by whom the offense came, shall we discern therein any de-

Allusion

Main Point III

Quotation

PERORATION STEP

parture from those divine attributes which the believers in a living God always ascribe to Him? Fondly do we hope, fervently do we pray, that this mighty scourge of war may speedily pass away. Yet, if God wills that it continue until all the wealth piled by the bondsman's two hundred and fifty years of unrequited toil shall be sunk, and until every drop of blood drawn with the lash shall be paid by another drawn with the sword, as was said three thousand years ago, so still it must be said, "The judgments of the Lord are true and righteous altogether."

With malice toward none, with charity for all, with firmness in the right as God gives us to see the right, let us strive on to finish the work we are in, to bind up the nation's wounds, to care for him who shall have borne the battle and for his widow and his orphan, to do all which may achieve and cherish a just and lasting peace among ourselves and with all nations.

THE DECLARATION

The declaration (of war, of national emergency, or of anything) follows much the same approach as the inaugural address. The legislative agent, whether congress or the people, is asked to ratify a situation already in existence. The reasons for seeking the declaration are magnified ("Yesterday, December 7, 1941, a day that will live in infamy, . . .") or the actions of the people making the declaration are praised ("The United States was at peace with that nation and . . . [was] looking toward the maintenance of peace in the Pacific."). The speaker recommends a line of action that is practical but undetailed. Events are allowed to speak for themselves, and the speaker does not try to prove or demonstrate the effectiveness of his action. He merely celebrates the idea that *something* must be done, and *declares* that his suggestion will be effective.

If the proposed action seems to fit the causative situation, ratification is usually automatic. Even in totalitarian nations, apparently, where the government is responsible only to itself, the declaration speech still must be made. The sample given below is well-known both as a moment of American history and as a typical "declaration of war."

GENERAL PURPOSE: To persuade.

SPECIFIC PURPOSE: To persuade the Congress of the United States that a state of war exists between the United States and the Empire of Japan.

PROPOSITION: Since the unprovoked and dastardly attack by Japan
                      on Sunday, December 7, 1941, a state of war has
                      existed between the United States and the Empire
                      of Japan.

TITLE: "War Message to Congress"*

TECHNICAL PLOT (What the speaker does)	OUTLINE (What the speaker says)
ATTENTION STEP Allusion	Yesterday, December 7, 1941—a date which will live in infamy—the United States of America was suddenly and deliberately attacked by naval and air forces of the Empire of Japan.
IDENTIFICATION STEP Sub-Point A Illustration Information	The United States was at peace with that nation and, at the solicitation of Japan, was still in conversation with its Government and its Emperor looking toward the maintenance of peace in the Pacific. Indeed, one hour after Japanese air squadrons had commenced bombing in the American Island of Oahu, the Japanese Ambassador to the United States and his colleague delivered to our Secretary of State a formal reply to a recent American message. And while this reply stated that it seemed useless to continue the existing diplomatic negotiations, it contained no threat or hint of war or of armed attack.
Sub-Point B Main Point I	It will be recorded that the distance of Hawaii from Japan makes it obvious that the attack was deliberately planned many days or even weeks ago. During the intervening time the Japanese Government has deliberately sought to deceive the United States by false statements and expressions of hope for continued peace.
Sub-Point A Information Information	The attack yesterday on the Hawaiian Islands has caused severe damage to American naval and military forces. I regret to tell you that very many American lives have been lost. In addition American ships have been reported torpedoed on the high seas between San Francisco and Honolulu.
Information	Yesterday the Japanese Government also launched an attack against Malaya.
Information	Last night Japanese forces attacked Hong Kong.
Information	Last night Japanese forces attacked Guam.
Information	Last night Japanese forces attacked the Philippine Islands.

*From *The Roosevelt Reader: Selected Speeches, Messages, Press Conferences, and Letters of Franklin D. Roosevelt*, ed. Basil Rauch (New York: Holt, Rinehart and Winston, 1957), pp. 300-301. Used by permission.

Information	Last night the Japanese attacked Wake Island.
Information	And this morning the Japanese attacked Midway Island.
Sub-Point B Allusion	Japan has, therefore, undertaken a surprise offensive extending throughout the Pacific area. The facts of yesterday and today speak for themselves. The people of the United States have already formed their opinions and well understand the implications to the very life and safety of our nation.
Main Point II	
Main Point III	As Commander-in-Chief of the Army and Navy I have directed that all measures be taken for our defense.
Main Point IV	But always will our whole nation remember the character of the onslaught against us.
Sub-Point A	No matter how long it may take us to overcome this premeditated invasion, the American people in their righteous might will win through to absolute victory.
Sub-Point B	I believe that I interpret the will of the Congress and of the people when I assert that we will not only defend ourselves to the uttermost but will make it very certain that this form of treachery shall never again endanger us.
Main Point V	Hostilities exist. There is no blinking at the fact that our people, our territory and our interests are in grave danger.
PERORATION STEP	With confidence in our armed forces—with the unbounding determination of our people—we will gain the inevitable triumph—so help us God.
Formal Proposition	I ask that the Congress declare that since the unprovoked and dastardly attack by Japan on Sunday, December Seventh, 1941, a state of war has existed between the United States and the Japanese Empire.

THE COMMENCEMENT ADDRESS

Every June in the United States it seems impossible to allow graduating students to leave school quietly. Whether in high school or college, the graduates must listen to a speech by an older person of some prominence, often a product of the institution involved, before they can receive their diplomas.

To someone under thirty (or to a faculty member listening year after year) this speech probably seems the most hackneyed and useless of all celebratory speeches. Yet there is no inherent reason why magnification of the social values that a school or college has tried to inculcate and a plea for creative use of the knowledge it has spread to the new "replacements" should be trite and worthless. Presumably the values of a student's society *are* "good." The speaker needs to perceive "what is truly felt" by his audience—the graduates—and to avoid speaking primarily to the parents and other "adults" who are present. Though he obviously must appease the people who have paid for the students' education, he must focus on the students themselves. His freshness is limited only by his ability to find a central idea close to the actual state of mind among the graduates. His eloquence is restricted only by his skill with the techniques of speech.

The proposition of a commencement address usually asks the students to practice the values or the knowledge they have acquired. The action called for is undetailed, and sometimes the proposal merely affirms the values or the knowledge. The points to be developed vary with the subject, of course. It is important, however, to use the experiences of the audience as a major source of illustrations and to make the proposition and the arguments as concrete as possible.

The following example is an imaginary speech prepared for an actual situation.

GENERAL PURPOSE: To persuade.

SPECIFIC PURPOSE: To persuade the graduates to use their knowledge and skill to aid mankind.

PROPOSITION: You should become involved in mankind.

TITLE: "The Paradox"

TECHNICAL PLOT (What the speaker does)	OUTLINE (What the speaker says)
ATTENTION STEP	Ladies and gentlemen:
ORIENTATION STEP Allusion	Anyone interested in paradox would enjoy himself this evening. The calmness—the gentle dignity—of this ceremony in the Sun Bowl clashes with the excitement of the new adventure we
Explanation Illustration	celebrate here. But El Paso itself—this university itself—is a paradox. In the middle of the desert we have a garden. Look around you at this
Allusion	luxuriant field of grass set down in a garden of rocks and sand. Look out below us to the valley
Allusion Allusion	where the farms and ranches sparkle in the sunshine. And think how a mere "pass to the north" has become a center of learning, of culture, and

	of industry—a place where people stop, and stay, rather than pass through.
Explanation	But the chief paradox is you, the class of 1968. The State of Texas, through its university, will soon announce that you are accredited bachelors or masters of arts and sciences, of engineering and education. Yet the ceremony today says that now you have finished, you are just "beginning."
Formal Purpose	It is this beginning—this commencement—that I want to talk about.
Association	I am assuming that—unlike the students in the old story Jonathan Swift told about Oxford, that it must be a great seat of knowledge because every freshman came there with it, but no senior ever took any of it away—*you* have acquired
Explanation	something tangible here. You can feel it even if you cannot define it. While your body and brain have aged four years, your mind and soul have grown several thousand years as a result of your immersion in the ideas and feelings, the knowledge and skill, of five thousand years of civilization.
Explanation	I am assuming, therefore, that you leave this university not as an American, not as a Texan, not even as a Miner—but as *men* and *women,* who are able to confront the problems of the twentieth
Partition	century and to perform skillfully both in your chosen field and in the much more difficult role of *citizen.*
(Transition)	(I do not have to tell you of the problems.)
ARGUMENTATION STEP Main Point I	You have been asked by your parents to ignore the problems of your time, by your government to die for them, and by your own leaders to solve them.
Illustration	You know that our cities are burning and bleeding, and the fire is fed and the blood is hurried by both the general indifference of our citizens and the massive federal, state, and local spending.
Illustration	You know that failing farms and businesses, chronic unemployment, and petrifaction of trade grow faster and faster in the midst of the greatest prosperity any people have ever known in the history of the world.
Illustration Association	You know that in Viet Nam, in China and in Southeast Asia, in Africa and the Middle East, war rages like one of our sandstorms.

Illustration Association	You know that the fruits of war and industry turn our rivers and seas into slime and bring the atmosphere down around us like a shroud.
Illustration	You know that America's largest and most successful businesses are those that build and sell products "unsafe at any speed" or poisonous to the air and seas around us; that change the packaging twenty-five times a year but the product never; and that resist with millions of dollars and words the establishment of truth in lending, truth in packaging, or safety in their products.
Illustration	You know that the "hard sell" or the "soft sell," the "gimmick," and control of your irrational impulses are more important to our hucksters and our politicians than all the values in the Ten Commandments, the Sermon on the Mount, or the Bill of Rights.
Illustration Allusion Association	You know that school principals, college presidents, liberals, conservatives, or radicals of right and left share one central concept today—all ideas but mine, all people but me, must burn at the stake—just as in Hitler's Germany on May 10, 1933, more than 25,000 books were cremated by screaming savages in hob-nailed boots.
Association Allusion Association	And how easily an idea gives up the ghost. If you stab it, it won't bleed. If you beat it, it won't bruise. If you burn it, it won't scream. It merely turns to smoke and ashes, and one morning you wake up to find the smell of death around you: dead ideas, dead minds, and a dead civilization. When we seek to purify our neighbor with the Nazi torch, we destroy ourselves first of all.
(Transition)	(No, I do not have to tell you the problems that await you when you leave this beautiful place. Nor do I want to ask you to solve them.)
Main Point II Quotation Allusion Allusion Quotation Explanation	Sophocles answered that plea when he wrote: "Look upon Oedipus. This is the king who solved the famous riddle and towered up, most powerful of men. No mortal eyes but looked on him with envy. Yet in the end ruin swept over him." But Sophocles also said that it is better to be dead than blind. And this evening I want to add that it is better to be blind than not to act—to become, in John Donne's elegant phrase, "involved in mankind." That means *first* the man to your right and to your left; *then* the town, the state, the country to the east and to the west, to the north and to the south. Whatever your major,

SUMMATION STEP

PERORATION STEP

whatever your job, whatever you do and where-ever you go, make their problems your profession.

"And therefore never send to know for whom the *bell* tolls; it tolls for *thee*." Do not abdicate your responsibility to make every city a garden, and every garden a boon to all mankind. Do not ig-nore the weak and the indigent, but do not seek to buy their souls with money. Do not enter into wars lightly, but being in them, seek victory with resolution and magnanimity. Do not accept the putrefaction of the air we breathe or the water we drink. Do not condone bigotry, lying in the press and advertisements, or shoddy practices in business or in government. Do not treat any per-son or group as a means rather than an end. Do not surrender to the sick and the profane your reason, your freedom, or your country. Do not locate evil outside yourselves alone, and do not burn ideas or people at the stake of barbarism.

For if you do, you might as well have never been born. No riddle can be completely solved, and little can be learned, but each of you can become something worthy to be remembered. Make your life a democracy, and fight and work to make that democracy live. Swear with Thomas Jeffer-son eternal war upon all tyranny over the minds of men. Take arms against the troubles that we bear. Involve yourself in mankind. "It tolls for *thee*."

THE SERMON

Like most counseling speeches, the sermon aims primarily at rein-forcement but also calls for a commitment on the part of its audience. The central idea is normally a pronouncement from the dogma of a particular religion. This directive is amplified in great detail and then applied to the present audience. The application is often laid in abstract or philosophical terms, such as "Strive to be a better Christian (Catholic, Protestant, etc.)." Or it can emphasize the relationship between the situation described in the dogma and the actual behavior of the people listening to the sermon. Without coming to grips with audience problems, the sermon nevertheless works to revitalize faith in a traditional attitude toward both the problems and their solutions. Since the central concepts of religion are matters of faith, it is vital that this faith be recharged from time to time.

On occasion the pulpit may be used to crystallize latent attitudes and beliefs around a practical line of action. In the American Revolution, for example, sermons led the way in reinforcing attitudes of rebellion. During the last two decades of the nineteenth century, ministers in America preached a social gospel much like the latter-day New Deal. The present controversy over the "God is dead" theology and the participation of the clergy in the civil rights movement probably indicates similar attempts to cause meaningful and practical action from the pulpit. Yet the resistance to the social gospel and the new theology (despite the success of the Revolutionary War preachers) no doubt reveals the communicants' primary desire for reinforcement of old beliefs without any hint of deliberation about new ones.

The sermon that appears below almost perfectly illustrates the traditional mixture of celebration with counseling.

GENERAL PURPOSE: To persuade.

SPECIFIC PURPOSE: To celebrate acceptance of Christ's offer of salvation through obedience to His Word.

PROPOSITION: We should accept Christ's offer of salvation through obedience to His Word.

TITLE: "The Great Disturber"*

TECHNICAL PLOT (What the speaker does)	OUTLINE (What the speaker says)
	TEXT: *Mark* 5:1-20
ATTENTION STEP	Twice before we have talked about this story. I keep being drawn back to it, and I believe this is because it provides one of the best illustrations of the gospel, namely, that God accepts the unacceptable and in this acceptance there is health and wholeness.
ORIENTATION STEP Formal Purpose	Today I would like to focus attention on the response of the demoniac, for he is our prototype, though, thank God, we are not quite as sick as he was. Need it be said that what the
Definition	scriptures describe as "demon-possession," modern medicine would call schizophrenia?
Explanation	However he is described, though, the demoniac *is* our prototype. His response is our response, his ambivalence is our ambivalence, and his ques-

---

*Delivered Sunday, October 16, 1966, by Reverend Gordon S. Bowie, Minister of the University Presbyterian Church, North Stanton at Gregory Way, El Paso, Texas. Used by permission.

tion—"What have you to do with me, Jesus?"—
is our question.

Quotation

My word, how ambivalent this man was! "And
when he had come out of the boat, there met
him out of the tombs a man with an unclean
spirit." That is, the demoniac made the first approach. Indeed we are told that he ran and wor-
shipped Jesus. Here is the attraction, but there
follows immediately the withdrawal, "What have
you to do with me, Jesus, Son of the Most High
God? I adjure you by God, do not torment me."
Here was a man at one and the same time
strangely attracted and strongly repelled by the
presence of Christ.

This ambivalence is in all of us. When we are
confronted by Christ, we too are attracted and
repelled. Sometimes the attraction predominates,
and we respond as did the demoniac. Sometimes
the repulsion predominates, and we respond like
the townspeople, who told Jesus to clear out of
it. In either case, we cannot ignore Him. He has
come to torment us. He has come to disturb us!

How?

Well, first and most obviously, he disturbs with
a demand for obedience. This both attracts and
repels us, as we all know. And we know further
that he makes this demand in every department
of life—in marriage, in the home, in education, in
industry, in commerce, in politics. Ah, but this
isn't always attractive, and more often than not
we respond not only with the demoniac—"What
have you to do with me, Jesus?"—but also with
the townspeople: "Get back to Galilee. Get back
to the church. Get back to the Bible. Get back
anywhere, but leave us alone." Often we want to
delineate the areas in which we will be obedient,
whereas Christ demands obedience in all areas
of life. Often our devotion is to a "way of life"
rather than to life itself, and when the way of
Christ conflicts with our way of life, we tell him
where to go.

A critic has drawn attention to a curious omis-
sion in the sermons of Jeremy Taylor, a well-
known British preacher of a former age. The
critic says: "These sermons are amongst the most
able and profound in the English language, but
they hardly ever mention the poor, hardly ever
refer to their sorrows, and show practically no

The margin labels (left column), aligned with the body text, read:

Quotation

Quotation

Restatement

Explanation

Formal Proposition

(Transition)

ARGUMENTATION STEP

Main Point I

Explanation

Repetition

Allusion

Restatement

Explanation
Allusion

Information

interest in their state. The sermons were preached in South Wales where poverty abounded. The cry of the poor and the hungry, the ill-clothed and the needy, ceaselessly ascended up to heaven, and called out for pity and redress, but their eloquent divine never seemed to hear it. He lived and wrote and preached surrounded by the suffering and the needy, and yet remained scarcely conscious of their existence."

Association

Contrast this with the attitude of a layman, Lord Shaftesbury. He had tried to get a bill through parliament to protect chimney sweeps, but had

Quotation

failed, so he wrote in his diary: "Very sad and low about the loss of the Sweeps Bill . . . but I must persevere and by God's help, so I will." Thirteen years later, when the bill was actually passed, he became aware of the appalling conditions under which women and children worked

Quotation

in factories, so he wrote: "The work to be done is greater than ever. But surely this career has been ordained to me by God and therein I rejoice, yea, and will rejoice."

Rhetorical Question

Which of these two men is closer to the mind and spirit of Christ? Not Jeremy Taylor, I should

(Transition)

think. And yet the attitude of Taylor is abroad in the church today.

Explanation

Now in saying this, I am not simply speaking to those of a conservative bent, but to all of us. For even if we agree that Christ demands more from us than a mere private morality, and don't attempt to meet His demands, we are not one whit better than the disciples of Taylor. We have to share in the church's guilt and failure. Repeatedly the church has sold Christ down the river. And

Rhetorical Question

what has happened? Who has replaced him? Why, Karl Marx and his "Communist Manifesto"

Explanation
Repetition

have provided the word of hope for the poor and the downtrodden in many lands. "What have you to do with me, Jesus, Son of the Most High

Restatement

God?" Christ disturbs us with the demand for obedience in every area of life. How will we

Rhetorical Question

respond? Will the attraction outweigh the repulsion?

(Transition)

But Christ disturbs us not only with the demand for obedience, but also with the gift for wholeness. Again, like the demoniac, we respond with ambivalence. He was reluctant to let go of his sickness and accept the offer of health. The same

Main Point II

reluctance is found in us. When we are offered

the gift of wholeness, we don't welcome it with open arms.

Why? At least two reasons present themselves.

Explanation

First, to be saved, to be restored to wholeness, we must recognize our need in all its dimensions. This acknowledgment is difficult and painful. It is easier to maintain our illusions about ourselves. The first step toward wholeness is to face the facts, and the facts are not pleasant.

Second, it is safer to maintain the status quo than to venture out into the unknown. The threat of the unfamiliar can be traumatic. We are always repelled by change and upheaval. Contrast, for example, the attitude of the white majority toward the negro riots the past two summers with that same majority's attitude toward the negro's participation in society during his first one hundred years of freedom. Look, for instance, at the number of Roman Catholics who are deeply disturbed by recent changes in doctrine made by the Vatican.

Association
Illustration

Illustration

These examples strike a responsive note in all of us, for we are all reluctant to give up what is known, what is familiar. The astonishing thing, in fact, is the length to which our passion for the familiar leads us to prefer sickness to health. We are not so different from the demoniac as we might suppose. We have the same ambivalence toward Christ, and the same reluctance to let go of it. This kind of inner division and hostility characterizes most of us most of the time. It is a commonplace in modern psychology that no absolute line can be drawn between the normal and the neurotic or psychotic individual. The man in the biblical story has an experience that he describes as being torn apart by a legion of demons. We still live in such a demon-haunted world. Men and women are torn apart by fear, worry, anxiety, insecurity, self-concern, and hostility—the same demons that haunted the man in the story.

Restatement

Association

Explanation

Association

Restatement

Oh, yes, we are all demon-possessed. We are all torn apart by forces we cannot control. But again, like the demoniac, we respond ambivalently and reluctantly to the offer of deliverance. One of the saddest things I see every day is people like those portrayed in the film "Who's Afraid of Virginia Woolf?" They are caught in a vicious circle of pain and suffering. They are caught in the vi-

Illustration
Association

Repetition	cious circle of mutual self-destruction. They go from one agony to another and make no attempt
Rhetorical Question	to leave the circle. May we not assume they do not want to leave it?
SUMMATION STEP	"What have you to do with me, Jesus, Son of the Most High God?" Christ disturbs us with a demand for obedience and an offer of wholeness. Only when we respond with all our being, only when we feel secure with God, does the world hold no terrors for us. Only when we respond to Jesus Christ without ambivalence and without reluctance do the demons of fear and worry and insecurity no longer plague us. Only when we renew ourselves in Christ every day of our lives can we let go of the demons that would haunt us.
PERORATION STEP Formal Proposition	Christ comes as the great disturber. He disturbs us with a demand and a gift. He demands obedience, and he offers wholeness. How will we respond? Like the townspeople, and remain sick? Or with the demoniac, and be healed?

THE NOMINATION SPEECH

The last speech of counsel to be studied in this chapter occupies a shadow-land between celebration and deliberation. On the one hand, the audience is much like that which comes to hear a sermon. The faithful gather to seek public communion with "The Infinite"—which in this case might be called "The Ghost of Elections Past."

On the other hand, the delegates also seek to deliberate about a candidate. The speaker faces a "problem-solution" situation much like that in the legislative assembly. The "problem" is the filling of an office. The "solution" is the speaker's desired candidate. The agent who will carry out the actions described in the party platform is himself a "recommended action."

As a rule, the speaker first delineates the requirements of the office. Then he describes his candidate in terms of the way he meets these requirements. The following nomination speech is based on several historical ones, but is itself imaginary. The actual speeches were each too long to fit this book. Brevity, it is sad to report, seldom rules at a nominating convention.

GENERAL PURPOSE: To persuade.

SPECIFIC PURPOSE: To celebrate the identification between Hubert Horatio Humphrey and the office of President of the United States.

PROPOSITION: Hubert Horatio Humphrey has proven his fitness for
                    the office of President of the United States.

TITLE: "Nomination of Hubert Horatio Humphrey"

TECHNICAL PLOT	OUTLINE
(What the speaker does)	(What the speaker says)

ATTENTION STEP

Mr. Chairman, Fellow Democrats, Fellow Americans:

IDENTIFICATION STEP

I rise to nominate the man who will be the next President of the United States. This is not a task I have taken lightly. The man who becomes our President carries on his shoulders all the prayers and hopes of a thousand million frightened and weary people. The dilemmas he must solve literally can mean life or death to all mankind.

Main Point I

It is not a job for weaklings, or for men of indecision. As Lyndon Baines Johnson has shown us, it is a job for courage, for integrity, for training, and for wisdom. It is above all else a job for a man who has *proven* he is capable of guiding our nation through the perilous years ahead.

Main Point II

Sub-Point A

Sub-Point B

Sub-Point C

Sub-Point D

Sub-Point E

Sub-Point F

In 1943, the man who is my choice for the awesome job of President assumed the leadership of a broken and defeated Democratic Party in Minnesota, and led it to a resounding victory. As Mayor of Minneapolis—as Senator from Minnesota—he led his state ahead of all others to establish a commission for fair employment, to inaugurate veterans' housing programs, and to achieve the first coalition of those farmers and laborers who are the backbone of our party and our country. From his first days in the Senate he was a leading Democratic spokesman in foreign and domestic affairs—a leader of his colleagues, and a colleague of the leaders. In 1948, six years before the Supreme Court decreed it was the law of the land and fifteen years before it became fashionable, he joined Harry S. Truman and Lyndon Baines Johnson in championing human rights for all our people. In 1960, he campaigned long and vigorously in support of John Fitzgerald Kennedy. In 1964, he was chosen by President Lyndon Baines Johnson to serve as his Vice-President. During his four years in this public trust, he has been the President's chief ambassador to Europe, to the Middle East, to Southeast Asia, and to the Far East. He was chosen by the President to lead our people out of the darkness of riot into the sunlit uplands of peace and plenty for all our citizens.

RATIONALIZATION STEP   But I do not have to continue. Ask the people of Minnesota, who gave him a ringing endorsement the first and every time he ran for public office. Ask his colleagues in the Senate, who made him their leader. Ask the delegates to this convention in 1964, who found in him the courage, the integrity, the training, and the wisdom of a president. Ask the President of the United States, who has personally trained Hubert Humphrey for the highest office our nation possesses.

PERORATION STEP   Ask yourselves if you want a man proven by twenty-five years of public service to lead when others only follow, to command when others only obey, to decide when others only hesitate. Ask yourselves if you want a man the people trust, a man who carries victory as his banner—the next President of the United States: Hubert Horatio Humphrey.

SUGGESTIONS FOR FURTHER READING

BERQUIST, GOODWIN F., JR. *Speeches for Illustration and Example.* Chicago: Scott, Foresman, 1965.

LINKUGEL, WIL A., R. R. ALLEN, and RICHARD L. JOHANNESEN. *Contemporary American Speeches: A Sourcebook of Speech Forms and Principles.* Belmont, Calif.: Wadsworth, 1965.

MARSHALL, PETER. *Mr. Jones, Meet the Master: Sermons and Prayers of Peter Marshall.* New York: Fleming H. Revell, 1949.

Chapter 7

IN CONCLUSION

Speechmaking requires an audience and a speaker. If you are the speaker, you will usually have a particular occasion and a specific audience to worry about. Your audience will have definite expectations about what you are supposed to accomplish. Though you must analyze each situation as if it had never occurred before, a number of similar situations continue to appear over and over. It is possible to isolate each of these basic types—inquiry and explanation, persuasion and deliberation, courtesy and sociality, commemoration, and counsel—and to study principles, techniques, and sample speeches for each situation.

In the preceding chapters we have examined both the characteristics of each situation and the strategy you may use to adapt to its demands. We have assumed that in every situation you must invent, arrange, phrase, and present *ideas* vocally, verbally, gesturally, and/or pictorially in a particular place at a particular time for the purpose of self-expression, group coordination, and social control. First you study audience and situation to discover what the means of communication should be. Then you analyze the *idea* you want to communicate. And finally you invent, arrange, phrase, and present the *ideas and images* you believe will satisfy the demands of the speech situation. It seems obvious that these demands are the primary forces controlling what you say and do.

The general character of these forces has been delineated chapter by chapter for each typical situation. As you prepare your speech for your own special occasion, knowledge of what other men have done on similar occasions will lighten your task.

Strange as it may seem, though the world today appears different from the worlds in the past, men still gather at speeches for the same five reasons apparent throughout history: to inquire into and explain their environment; to evaluate and deliberate their problems and solutions; to ease their social interaction; to commemorate their special occasions; and to seek counsel and guidance. The world is certainly more dangerous today, but *man* is still *speechmaking man*. Talking-it-through is still his best answer to the storms that beset him, particularly those he brings down upon himself. Only with great travail have men over the centuries learned ways of structuring their verbal confrontations. Like the speakers and students of earlier times, you can profit from studying what has been learned about the typical speech situations. Only today the stakes are incalculable.

INDEX